THE
TRADITIONAL
ARCHITECTURE
OF INDONESIA

THE
TRADITIONAL
ARCHITECTURE
OF INDONESIA

BARRY DAWSON • JOHN GILLOW

With 244 illustrations, 192 in color

THAMES AND HUDSON

For Teresa

Acknowledgments

Our thanks to: Mark Alston, Najib Dawa, Sarah Davies and Jeremy Levy, Format (Bradford), Fuji Film, Gabriel Photographic (Bradford), Alastair Hull, Ilford U.K., Professor Kam-Ching Leung, the School of Art, Design and Textiles, Bradford and Ikley Community College, Bernard Sellato, Bryan Sentance, Alan Smith, Ferdinand Swart, Bart van Ooteghem, Andrew Vaines, Warrens Photolabs (Leeds) and Adrian Young, for all their help. We would also like to acknowledge the works of Bernard Sellato, Roxana Waterson, J. A. Feldman, Lim Jee Yuan and J. Dumarcay, to whose scholarship we are much indebted.

All colour photographs are by Barry Dawson, with the exception of the following: 190, 192 by Maggie Gowan; 119-23 by Bernard Sellato.

All line drawings are by Bryan Sentance.

Title page
A carved wooden door panel from Jogjakarta, Java, depicting horses flanking the tree of life.

Contents

Introduction:
Tradition and Change

INDONESIAN CULTURE is steeped in tradition. The customs and beliefs, social organization, vernacular art and crafts of this vast archipelago have developed over many centuries, evolving in harmony with the natural environment and the rhythms of daily life. Despite the diversity of its peoples – spread over the 13,000 islands that stretch some 3500 miles in an arc from the north-west tip of Sumatra to the jungles of Irian Jaya – Indonesian society as a whole displays a remarkable cultural unity, which centres around a deeply held belief in the world of spirits. Its architecture has developed to cope not only with the climate and the natural hazards of the land, but also with the intangible realms of animistic mythology. The result is some of the most remarkable and spectacular vernacular building in the world.

The peoples of the archipelago are often materially rich and of great cultural sophistication. With a few exceptions, such as the inhabitants of Irian Jaya, they belong to the Austronesian language group whose members can be found as far afield as Madagascar and Taiwan. Strong similarities exist among the far-flung Austronesians, particularly in their material culture, their textiles and their domestic architecture.

The Indonesians who, outside populous Java and Bali, inhabit the rugged interiors of the main islands and most of the outlying islands, are known collectively as the 'ancient peoples' and, until recently, lived in cultural isolation. Their megalithic, often head-hunting societies reach back to the Dong-Son culture of the Annam region of north Vietnam, which was driven into Indonesia and other parts of South-East Asia between the eighth and second centuries BC as a result of military pressure from China. Their bronze kettle-drums, traded all over the archipelago, were covered in bas-relief motifs, prominent amongst which was a stilted boat-shaped wooden house with great upsweeping ridge ends. Variations of this ancient prototype constitute the predominant style of domestic architecture among the Batak of Sumatra and the Toraja of Sulawesi. The houses of these animist and conservative societies form some of the world's most impressive traditional architecture.

The Indonesian islands are spread across the trade routes between China to the north-east and India, Arabia and Europe to the north-west. To the coast of Sumatra, the Kalimantan and Sulawesi littorals, and Java, Madura and Bali – regarded by many as the heartlands of the Indonesian peoples – invaders, colonizers, missionaries, merchants and traders brought cultural changes that have had pronounced effects on building styles and techniques, and on the layout and orientation of villages. The most pervasive of these influences was that of India. India had established trading links with the coastal peoples of Java by the second century AD, and by the fifth century a Hindu kingdom had been founded; the kingdom of Srivijaya grew up in south Sumatra in the seventh century. Srivijaya, situated around modern Palembang, later became a major centre of Mahayana Buddhism, and its political influence was to be felt right up through the Malayan peninsula as far away as modern Thailand. The Javanese kingdom of Mataram assumed regional power in the mid-ninth century, and it was here that a fusion of Indian Buddhism, Hinduism and Javanese animistic religions engendered an architectural style that was manifested in the glorious structures of Borobudur, Prambanan and the temples of the Dieng plateau.

The influence of Indian culture is also evident in the mandala-like grouping of houses in villages in Java and Bali. Here, and in the settled parts of Sumatra, the villagers' labour and agricultural produce would have served the needs of the palaces, cities and the religious establishments. Although these large, Indian-style constructions were of stone, the villages would have been built of wood.

The Chinese were another major influence on Indonesian culture. Initially they came as traders, bringing silk and exquisite Ming porcelain so esteemed in the archipelago, later settling predominantly on the coasts of Sumatra, Java, Kalimantan and Sulawesi as miners, labourers and shopkeepers. Their effect on Indonesian domestic architecture was not so profound, however, being limited mainly to carpentry techniques, although it is likely that the longhouses of Borneo were inspired by Chinese bazaar architecture.

Islam came to Indonesia in the fifteenth century, by way of Muslim traders from Gujarat. Aceh, at the northern tip of Sumatra, was the first area to be converted. Islam spread rapidly through Sumatra, coastal Borneo and Sulawesi and into Java, bringing to an end the Hindu-Buddhist era on the islands and leading to the fall of the Majapahit Empire and the flight of the Javanese aristocracy to the safety of Bali.

The Europeans were the next interlopers. The Portuguese first reached the Moluccas at the beginning of the sixteenth century, but by 1600 the Dutch East India Company had taken over the trade with the archipelago and had begun the process of turning itself into the ruling colonial power. The Dutch, like the Chinese, lived in the cities in ground-based buildings in extremely insanitary conditions. For more than two centuries they did little to adapt their European habits to the tropical climate, surrounding themselves with canals, which provided ideal breeding grounds for the anopheles mosquito, and then dumping them full of noxious rubbish and sewage. Epidemics of malaria and dysentery were rife. Batavia (now Jakarta), the capital of the Dutch East Indies, consequently became the most unhealthy city in the Orient. The average life expectancy of a

Dutch colonial soldier stationed there was no more than a year; and it was after his stop in Batavia that Captain Cook lost nearly half his crew from sickness, on the return leg of his circumnavigation of the globe.

The Dutch had little direct effect upon most indigenous Indonesian building styles, although the balconies of the spectacular houses of the hill villages of south Nias were supposedly inspired by the bulbous sterns of the old Dutch galleons sent on punitive raids against the slave-trading and head-hunting Nias islanders. The Islamic influence was more pervasive, not so much in terms of structure but more in the way living accommodation was divided between the sexes. The front, public, parts of the house in the Malay-influenced areas, for instance, became the male domain. Women were restricted to the rear, though Malay women, as with the matrilineal Minangkabau of Sumatra where the same restrictions applied, were very often the actual owners of the house and land. This policy of sexual segregation is still observed, as can be seen from new converts in the Bima region of Sumbawa.

A riverside kampung, *a group of wooden houses raised on piles and thatched with palm leaf.*

The Indonesian village is the most important basic unit of economic and political life. Settlements would have originally developed from a core of related people located in proximity to food resources or trade facilities, and in former times fortified villages were built on isolated hilltops. One of the first steps taken by the colonizing Dutch was to force the belligerent Toraja of Sulawesi down from their fortified eyries to more easily policeable villages in the valleys.

As with the vast majority of the world's housing, most Indonesian dwellings are not architect-designed; the designation of roles into architect, builder and client is a phenomenon of industrialized society. A villager will build his own house, or else the whole community will work on a construction under the direction of a master-builder. Experienced carpenters also play a part in the building of traditional housing.

Each of the many Indonesian ethnic groups has its own distinctive form of traditional house. These houses are known as *rumah adat*, and are the symbolic centre of a web of customs, social relations, traditional laws, taboos, myths and religions that bind the villagers together. The house provides the main focus for the family and its community, and is the point of departure for the many different activities of its residents.

As the house forms the centre of social and religious life, it will be consecrated and undergo periodic cleansing rituals, as will the village as a whole. Beyond the village perimeters lies the outside world, the realm of uncontrolled spiritual forces. Images of guardian spirits are placed within and around the houses, at the entrances to the village and even among the crops, to ward off evil. Some parts of the house, therefore, are not structurally essential, but are decorative elements that have a cultural function. Rafters, pillars and roof friezes are frequently carved or painted with talismanic symbols and spirit imagery, especially in the remoter communities.

Building has evolved to cope with the equatorial conditions of the islands, their hot and humid but even daytime temperature and their very heavy monsoon rains (over most of the archipelago the lack of an extended dry season ensures the continuous growth of vegetation). The Indonesian *rumah adat* has a post-and-lintel structure with wooden or bamboo walls and a thatched roof, and all over Indonesia, with the exception of Java and Bali, houses are traditionally built on stilts.

Stilts are often quite tall and can either be set directly into the ground (as is the case with the giant ironwood pillars used in Borneo or on the Mentawai islands) or, more commonly, rest upon flat foundation stones. This has many advantages for life in a monsoon climate, raising the house to a height at which the cooling upper breezes can penetrate and away from the rain muds, and providing excellent underfloor ventilation in the hot weather. Tall piles lift the inhabitants free from most of the malaria-carrying mosquitoes and in the more troubled times of

A woman weaving cloth on a backstrap loom outside a traditional pile-built house, in the 1920s.

A 1930s riverside village. The same scene can be seen today, though the building materials have changed; the roofs, for instance, will now be of zinc.

the past would have added to the security of the house. Foundation stones allow the pile-built houses resting on them to move without damage during earth tremors (Indonesia is an extremely active earthquake zone); they are also much less affected by dry rot and termites than those set directly into the ground. The Toba Batak of Sumatra and the Toraja of Sulawesi give the substructure of their houses added stability by mortising a system of beams into the piles, thereby also creating night-time stalls for their cattle.

Traditional houses are renowned for their dramatically inclined roofs, which allow the vast amounts of tropical rainwater to run swiftly and safely away, and the overhanging eaves shade the windows and protect them from the driving rain. In the hot, humid coastal areas inhabited by people such as the Acehnese and the Bugis, houses usually have plenty of windows. Over much of the archipelago, however, the peoples living in the colder hills occupy houses whose walls are dwarfed by a vast roof, and will have few, if any, windows.

The wall in many traditional Indonesian forms of building is insignificant compared to the roof, whose great weight is supported by piles. The Bataks and Minangkabau of Sumatra and the Toraja of Sulawesi live in houses whose sharply sloping roof ridge ends curve dramatically upwards like the prow and stern of a boat. Houses with steeply inclined roofs can also be found in parts of

Nusa Tenggara (the chain of islands lying to the east of Bali), Sulawesi and Borneo, famous for its Dayak longhouses.

Buildings are usually of wood – hardwood for the piles and soft- and hardwoods for the upper part of the house, but coconut wood and bamboo are frequently used for the non-loadbearing elements. They are thatched with leaves from the sugar, coconut and other palms, *alang-alang* grass and rice straw; the variety of palm will depend on altitude and ecological zone. From the beginning of the twentieth century, however, zinc roofs have largely replaced thatch. An ingenious combination of joints, wedges, pegs and lashing ensures a sturdy yet flexible structure needing no nails. This has two main advantages: firstly, by removing the wedges, the buildings can be dismantled easily, and reassembled at a new location (with enough labour, in fact, the house can be lifted bodily off its foundation stones); and secondly, this type of jointed wooden building is better able to withstand earthquakes.

The architecture of houses built to the Malay model, such as those in Aceh, Jambi, Palembang, Bengkulu, Lampung and Riau in Sumatra, and that of the Bugis, Minahasans and other coastal inhabitants of Sulawesi, is less dramatic but conforms to the same broad configuration of stilts, steep roofs, and overhanging

The verandah of a Kenyah Dayak longhouse in cental Borneo. Men sit and socialize in this communal space. Trophy skulls hang above them, and against the walls lean ceremonial gongs and fishing tackle.

Children outside a Malay house. Modern houses of this type are little changed in design, and retain the steeply pitched roof and windows that are ideally suited to the hot, humid climate.

eaves. Malay houses have large, open interior spaces with only a few partitions. They are light and airy, and are characterized by their lightweight structure, abundance of shuttered windows and palm-leaf thatched roofs. Malay houses make good use of low thermal-capacity building materials and have evolved a variety of means to control heat and ventilation. A prefabricated building system has been developed for the Malay house, as has a very sophisticated extension scheme, which allows it to be enlarged to suit the growing needs of its occupants.

Houses derived from the Dong-Son prototype persisted in Java until the thirteenth century, but the model upon which the current Javanese houses are based was established in the Majapahit era of the fourteenth century. This is not built on piles, but on the ground, sometimes set on a masonry foundation. The simplest houses consist of one rectangular room with a mud floor and walls made up of a rigid matting of split bamboo, which are fixed from the inside onto the pillars that support the roof covering. Roof shapes vary regionally, but most commonly the central portion has four sides bordered with shallow eaves. The advantage of the Javanese ground plan is that the house can be easily extended.

In Bali, housing consists of a series of small constructions grouped together within the same compound. They mostly consist of wooden pillars raised on a masonry base, which support a roof structure of radiating beamwork, covered by thatch, tiles or bamboo. More rarely, the walls are built of brick or volcanic tuff masonry, but are still set on the same kind of foundation, and have the same style of roofing. Roofs are invariably crowned with a terracotta finial. The domestic architecture of the Balinese parts of Lombok is ground-built, similar to that of Bali. In both cases, buildings are richly decorated with floral patterning. The Sasaks of Lombok, however, traditionally live in ground-built thatched houses set on two levels.

Rumah adat in many parts of the archipelago rely on the natural unadorned beauty of their materials for their aesthetic effect. Elsewhere, houses are decorated with painting and wood-carving, the finest of which can be found adorning the magnificent walls and roofs of the Batak and Toraja. Often, as in the case of the Toraja and to a lesser extent the Batak, the size of the interior room surmounted by these great roofs is in fact very small. Unlike its Western counterpart, Indonesian domestic architecture does not aim to provide comfortable living space. Indeed, the interiors of Indonesian houses are often dark, cramped and smoky. The Indonesian home is a place for sleeping in, as most of the day will be spent out of doors. As well as providing protection from the elements and from predators, it houses the family's sacred heirlooms, which preserve cultural identity, and social continuity and hierarchy.

Many of the most elaborate traditional houses of the *orang asli*, the 'ancient peoples', are the 'houses of origin', built by the founding ancestor of a clan. The general word for 'house' in the Toraja language is *banua,* but the term for a house of origin is *tongkonan*, which is derived from the word meaning 'seat'. An Indonesian's place in society is of the utmost importance, so much so that in Bali, with its strictly stratified hierarchy, the perennial way to ascertain a newcomer's status is to ask 'Where do you sit?'. The Toraja house affects the life of its people most deeply. It is considered to be the seat of the revered ancestor who founded the house. One of his descendants presides over it and all the ceremonies for which it is the focus.

Ancestor worship is the central cultural and religious practice pervading the societies of the outer islands. Ancestors are believed to be able to mediate between the world of spirits and the material world, and are fundamental to tribal society in South-East Asia. They can be either protective or harmful, depending on the circumstances of their death and their treatment after death. Ancestors who died violently or childless, or whose ritual offerings have been neglected, may turn into malignant spirits, bringing bad luck, disease and infertility to their descendants and their crops and livestock. The most common major offerings to ancestors are great feasts, which are held at the burials that take place throughout tribal South-East Asia, and entail the mass-slaughter of pigs, chickens and buffalo. The supreme offering to a dead ancestor was once a human sacrifice, the death of a slave or captive, or a head taken in battle.

The Indonesian house provides the location not only for rituals, but also for working, cooking and sleeping, while at the same time securing a domain separate from the surrounding wilderness with all its attendant dangers. The division of the house according to function, and between areas for men and women, is prescribed both by practicality and by social and religious custom; as in other parts of South-East Asia, however, the division of the house is also an embodiment of local concepts of the cosmos. The house is seen as a microcosm and, like the universe itself, is vertically stratified into heaven, earth and the underworld, its orientation determined by the cardinal points or its proximity to the sea or the mountains.

The chief's great house, the *omo sebua*, at Bawomataluo village in south Nias, is divided into three levels: the lower level formed by the great piles on which the house stands is inhabited by pigs, the middle level provides the living space, and the upper level comprises the rafters, where the precious heirlooms are stored. The levels of the house are also thought to represent a range of different themes, including the division of society into slaves, commoners and nobility, the lower, middle and upper world of the Indonesian cosmos, and the human body: the stilts are the legs of the house, the roof is the top of its head and the arms are the two pillars of the main room (the pillars are positioned irregularly, a characteristic also found in the architecture of the Karo Batak, the Ngaju Dayak of Kalimantan and the Atoni of Timor). Even the ventilation flap in the roof is supposed to be a curl on the top of a child's head. The entrance to the chief's house is

An uma *(communal longhouse) of the 1920s, built by the Sakuddei tribe of Siberut island, off the west coast of Sumatra.*

a gangway that threads its way between the pillars. Midway along this gangway is a staircase that leads up to a trap door opening into the main room. This trap door is known as the navel of the house. The inside is adorned with carvings of bracelets, clothing, headgear and weapons and other ceremonial attire.

Indonesia's rural population is mainly distributed into villages that are characteristically conservative, and emphasize the continuing rapport of man and nature. Before late nineteenth-century colonial interference, the scope of human knowledge was regarded as foreordained by supernatural powers and the original stock of ideas was considered to be absolute, not to be expanded, questioned or altered. Consequently, planning solutions in these hitherto isolated societies remained unchallenged until this time, but in the early twentieth century, one of the effects of the Dutch colonial rulers' new ethical policy, for instance, was the enforced destruction of the great communal houses of the Manggarai people of

A Balinese girl bringing offerings to a temple. The walls of the twin towers are built of brick faced with profusely carved paras. *This soft stone perfectly lends itself to the intricate style of Balinese carving, which still continues today.*

Toba Batak dignitaries outside their juba *(ancestral home) on Samosir Island, Sumatra.*

west Flores, for fear that their crowded, smoke-filled interiors led to tuberculosis and promiscuity, and the rotting rubbish in the middens below caused disease.

The independence of all Indonesia was finally gained from the Dutch by 1950, followed by years of political confusion, secessional revolt and economic chaos, which at last came to an end in 1965. The stability then provided by President Suharto's military government has allowed the abundant natural riches of the Indonesian islands to flourish. Economic development has had major effects on construction in Indonesia's traditional societies. Because of the great improvements in transportation and the enormously increased economic activity of the major cities, there has been mass immigration of the 'ancient peoples' from their traditional homelands into Jakarta, Surabaya, Ujung Pandang, Medan and even Kupang on Timor, which has seen an influx of people from the neighbouring islands of east Nusa Tenggara. Though this process of urbanization has of course exacted its toll, the different ethnic groups in these large Indonesian cities have mostly held on to their cultural identity through grouping together in certain quarters of town. Although housing styles in the towns will conform to the current urban norm – ground-built bungalows, two- or three-storey buildings, or shacks built of wood, concrete, glass and corrugated iron or ceramic tiles – one of the characteristic features of the Western-style public buildings is the way in which elements of local traditional architecture such as saddle roofs or finials in the shape of buffalo horns are incorporated into them, sometimes using the old building methods. The migrants are ever mindful of their homeland, spending the savings they have accrued back in their ancestral villages. The Toba Bataks build great concrete tombs for themselves in the boat-shape of the traditional Toba house, and the Minangkabau erect profusely carved clan houses with their many gabled roofs. The Toraja construct modern European-style bungalows to live in with new but traditionally fashioned *tongkonan* or rice barns set beside them. The same process applies to all the other migrant groups from the different tribes of Indonesia. Further funds for new building are available in areas that attract large numbers of tourists, such as Bali, Tana Toraja and Lake Toba, and of course traditional building in its turn lures yet more tourists.

Traditional housing forms still constitute a very large percentage of Indonesia's housing stock, and in many of the most culturally conservative societies of the archipelago, they still have a vitally important talismanic role, both as storehouses for sacred heirlooms and as centres for ritual celebrations. Although a new *rumah adat* is now no longer inaugurated by placing newly taken heads at each corner of a room, a massive feast will still be given by the founder, with pigs and buffalo providing meat for all who laboured on the house. The feasting turns the house into a spiritual entity and the founder into a living ancestor, ensuring that cosmic harmony, so essential to the Indonesian well-being, will prevail.

Below *A woman and child standing in the courtyard of their home in pre-war Sulawesi. The frame, wall panels and even the windows are of bamboo; the roof is of palm-leaf thatch.*

Below, right *Villagers sitting outside a simple rural house in central Java in the 1920s. Many houses like this are still found today, though they will have tiled roofs and more durable walls.*

On the other hand, however, traditional *rumah adat* are being replaced throughout Indonesia by houses built to the contemporary Javanese model, with brick and cement walls and zinc roofs. This is because it is usually cheaper to build, and increasingly appeals to Indonesian villagers who are succumbing to the attractions of the dominant Javanese culture, which are reinforced by television and film and compounded by the effect of progressive government propaganda. Villagers in the more remote parts of the archipelago have largely discarded or are in the process of discarding their indigenous animist religion and adopting Christianity or Islam. The abandonment of the *rumah adat* with its often communal living arrangements and its now disparaged cultural associations is actively encouraged by missionaries of all persuasions.

These two opposing forces of modernism and conservatism seem to be moving towards a resolution, whereby the traditional *rumah adat* is conserved and in many cases renovated, either with the help of remittances from wealthy emigrants or through access to newly available tourist revenue. The majority of the villagers now live in single family units in their own local version of contemporary Javanese housing, but will continue to preserve and sometimes build afresh *rumah adat*, to maintain the vital link between themselves and their ancestors and to express the natural pride they feel in their own native culture.

1
Materials and Construction

TRADITIONAL ARCHITECTURE is a product of its environment; each regional variant develops in response to the conditions and materials determined by the local climate and vegetation. Within Indonesia lies one of the largest remaining ranges of rain forest, second only to Amazonia in area and importance to world ecology. For the Indonesian villagers, the forest supplies softwood and hardwood, bamboo, rattan and a diverse range of palm woods, which are readily available in many parts of the archipelago. Even in the densely populated islands of Java and Bali, which have lost most of their forest cover, building timber can be bought in from the saw mills of Kalimantan at affordable rates.

The giants of South-East Asia and the dominant species of the forests are the *Dipterocarpaceae*, a large family of trees with massive, often buttressed trunks. They predominate in the lowland rain forests of Sumatra, Malaya and Borneo and what little remains of the forest in Java, making them the tallest rain forests in the world. Known locally as *keruing* or *meranti*, these trees have trunks that are ideal for timber: they are self-pruning, their wood is hard but light, and most species can be easily floated down river; but sadly, these qualities have meant that they are now being felled at a rate that cannot be sustained. *Dipterocarpaceae* constitute most of the timber exports of Indonesia and Malaysia. Water, however, seems to hinder their propagation, and most *Dipterocarpaceae* are not found east of the Straits of Makassar, which separate Borneo from Sulawesi.

The king of the forest is the *Eusideroxylon zwageri*, the ironwood tree of the *Lauraceae* family, found in Sumatra and Borneo. Ironwood has extemely dense, very hard wood. The majestic and intimidating houses of south Nias and the Dayak longhouses of central Borneo are both raised on great ironwood pillars. All through Borneo, where there are more ironwood trees remaining than in Sumatra, they are used for floors, jetties, house posts, steps and walkways. Ironwood is even used for the hulls of canoes and *prahu* (boats).

Ironwood timber will endure for up to 150 years, and is impervious to insect attack – old timbers from decaying houses are often reused in new construction. Though extremely hard, it splits easily and is used as an alternative to teak to make the thin pentagonal tongue-shaped shingles that adorn the roofs of so many of the prestigious public buildings of Indonesia.

Bornean ironwood grows very slowly; indeed, a tree with a one-metre diameter trunk can take up to two hundred years to grow. Mature trees can attain a height of nearly 28 metres (90 ft). Ironwood trees grow in the lowland areas below 600 metres (about 2000 ft) and flourish on well-drained soils. The thickest stands used to be found on flat land by rivers. Unfortunately, this made them easy prey for the logging industry, for though ironwood trees are unusual in that they sink in water, loggers will tie them to lighter trees that act as floaters to take them down river. Ironwood is now rare. There are very few ironwood trees left in the still vast rain forests of Sumatra. They were logged out in west Kalimantan by 1925 and are now only to be found in the nature reserves of east and central Kalimantan, where even there they are vulnerable to illegal felling.

Cengal (*Balonocarpus heimii*) is another dark wood once much used in construction in Sumatra, but now only found in the Malayan peninsula. It, too, contains oils that help it resist termites. Jakfruit and breadfruit trees belong to the *Artocarpus* genus. Of rain-forest origin, they grow best in hot, wet climates and are semi-deciduous. Their leaves change colour slightly and drop from the trees at regular intervals. Both are valuable hardwoods used mainly for walls and interiors. The *Auracaria* conifer is found in New Guinea and is used by the Dani and the Yali of the Baliem valley of Irian Jaya to build the walls of their huts and the stockades that protect their compounds.

Teak (*Tectona grandis*) is another tree ideal for forestry. It is tall and straight with very few spreading branches and sparse laurel-shaped leaves. Easy to fell, it grows fast and its wood is hard and resistant to rot and insect attack. It can be found in plantations all over southern Asia, and is one of the most desirable woods for house construction. East and central Java have many teak plantations. Ebony, however, has always been scarce, and is now hardly ever used in building, although it was once used for the wall panels and interior carvings of the major houses of south Nias.

A range of palm trees proliferates all over the archipelago. They are mainly exploited for their fruits, their starch and sugar content and the shade they provide. Tapping for sugar is done by bruising a young inflorescence, leaving it for a few days and then collecting the sugary liquid exuded. Palms are an extremely valuable source of secondary building material. Their trunks are used in house frames in the absence of better timber, and their leaves are second only to *alang-alang* grass as a popular source of thatch.

The sugar palm (*Arenga dinnata*) is known locally as either *enau* or *kabong*. It is a massive solitary palm growing up to 18.5 metres (60 ft) tall with a deep blackish crown of numerous plume-like leaves. The black fibre that hangs onto the trunk in a tough, fibrous, highly resistant sheath is an important building material. Known as *ijuk,* it is the toughest form of thatch available. The Minangkabau thatch their beautiful *rumah gadang* with it and the thatch is said to last a hundred years. *Borassus* is known as the *lontar* palm in the Malay region, but usually as the palmyra palm elsewhere. There are more of these palms in the world than any other species with the exception of the coconut. Widely distributed, this solitary-fan palm can grow as tall as the sugar palm, and has a dense blue crown and stiff joined leaves that project in all directions. *Borassus* thrives in a monsoon climate, and grows wild east of Java. It is a prodigious source of sugar and toddy, giving off over fifty litres of sweet sap a week, and has become the economic foundation of such otherwise desolate islands as Rote and Savu, providing food, drink, sugar and pig fodder. Before the Portuguese introduced the technique of paper-making from wood fibre, records were written on strips of *lontar* palm leaf known as *ola*. The leaves of the *lontar* palm are still used to make buckets, baskets and thatch. The trunk is used for timber. The older the tree, the harder its trunk and the better it is for building, enabling young, productive trees to survive unscathed. The male tree is reputed to have darker, harder wood than the female.

The coconut tree, *Cocos nucifera*, is probably nature's greatest gift to man. Known to the islanders as *kelapa*, it is a tall solitary palm, often with a curving

Carved wooden grave doors of the Sa'dan Toraja of Sulawesi. The human figure represents the deceased, and the pattern of crosses surrounding him is derived from old Indian trade textiles. The carved buffalo head symbolizes virility, wealth and status.

trunk. Found in abundance, it grows well on sandy soils and in coastal regions. Coconut wood is used for houseposts and rafters (their durability is improved by soaking the wood in salt water first). Cords made from coir, a material derived from the husk of the coconut, may be used as lashing in house construction. Coconut wood, however, is full of silica and consequently blunts tools very quickly.

The sago palm (*Metroxylon sagu*), known as *rumbia* in Malay, is native to the Moluccas and to north-west New Guinea. Its profuse spread of leaves is a major source of thatch, which can last up to seven years before it needs renewing. Whereas sago palms generally grow inland, the *nipa* palm (*Nypa fruticans*) is found on the coasts. Its leaves also make very good thatch. The *nibung* palm (*Oncosperma tigillarium*) grows well in the Riau archipelago. It yields one of the hardest woods known, and is frequently used for scaffolding in Singapore.

There are nine species of rattan (from the Malay word *raut,* meaning 'to pare'), of which most can be found in Borneo and Sumatra. The rattans are a specialized group of scaly fruited palms, which have exploited their rain-forest environment by developing into giant climbers, with stems sometimes as thick as a man's arm and about 100 metres (325 ft) long. All possess two essential features, scaly fruits and springy leaf sheaths. Spines are long and strong, and have, in many species, developed into claw-like hooks. These palms were able to attach themselves to the surrounding plants with their comb-like plates of spines or with the backs of their leaf sheaths. All climbing rattans in Asia have long clawed leaf-tip whips. *Daemonorops* is the second biggest genus of rattans, and is especially concentrated in Sumatra, the Malayan peninsula and Borneo. *Plectocomia* is the giant mountain rattan found in Sumatra, Java and Borneo.

Rattans are principally a source of cane, which, centuries ago, Chinese entrepreneurs were quick to exploit. The sources of commercial rattan are Sumatra, Riau and Kalimantan. In house-building, rattan is mainly used as a material for lashing house timbers together. Rattan canes can be woven into house panels and the leaves used for thatch.

There are more than seven hundred species of bamboo in the world, and approximately half grow in South-East Asia. Clumps of bamboo, some of great height and girth, are to be found all over Indonesia. They provide a ready, light and sustainable source of building material. The trunk or stem of bamboo is known as the culm, which is made up of hollow cavities, separated from each other by diaphragms, which appear on the outside of the culm as nodes, the points at which the branches leave the culm. The section of culm between two nodes is called an internode. Bamboo grows by extending each internode upwards from the base. Very fast growth is normal, as each of the twenty or more internodes are all growing at the same time. On average a bamboo culm can grow 30 centimetres (one foot) a day.

Detail of the roof cladding of a Toraja traditional house. Sections of bamboo are bound together with rattan and assembled transversely in layers to cover the roof.

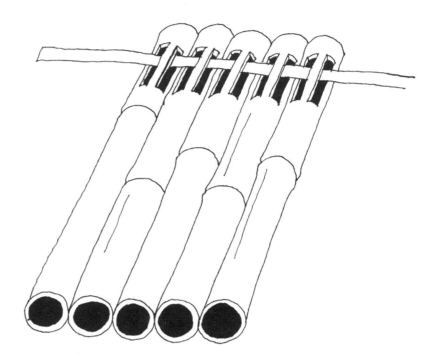

As building material, bamboo has many advantages. Because its culm is hollow, it is relatively strong and stiff and can be cut and split easily with simple tools (although the outer skin of the culm contains a lot of silica, which quickly dulls their edges). It has a hard, clean surface. Bamboo may cultivated in Indonesia as a crop, or it can easily be collected from the wild, making it cheap and readily available. Very importantly for Indonesia, bamboo structures have been shown to endure storm and earthquake well. Bamboo is not very durable, however, and can hardly withstand contact with wet soil. It is also very vulnerable to termite attack. Standardization is virtually impossible, since bamboo is not straight but tapered and occurs in widely differing sizes; the nodes also occur at irregular intervals. Bamboo constructions are also flammable. The culms are stiff, bending only so far and then failing (if not overly stressed, bamboo will return to its original shape). The hollow tubes of the culms and their sometimes thin walls make them harder to join together than pieces of wood, but they have no rays or knots and are easily replaceable.

In such areas as central Flores, where bamboo grows in profusion, many of the houses are made from it almost exclusively, and it comprises much of the construction material of poorer houses and temporary structures all over the archipelago. Walls and inner partitions are very often of interwoven split bamboo, and decorative patterns are achieved by contrasting the shiny outer surface of the culm with the duller inner surface. Sometimes wall and floor panels are made simply out of sections of culm that have been split vertically, the diaphragms removed and the whole hollow section flattened out to form a rectangular panel. Floors can be made in this manner, or of interwoven splits or indeed of strips of bamboo sewn together. More usually, floors are made entirely of whole culms laid side by side resting on joists. They all have a characteristic springiness.

All over Indonesia, bamboo culms are used for framing members, for joists, rafters, purlins and often for the ridge pole itself. Whole or half rounds of bamboo can be used for roof tiling. Half rounds can be interlocked alternately, one convex side down, then one up. When bamboo is used for the house or roof frame, the virtue of its lightness means that whole sections can be prefabricated on the ground and then installed at leisure.

Bamboo is also used as scaffolding, even in big cities: it clings incongruously to the soaring skyscrapers in the modern metropolis of Singapore. Because of its limited durability, bamboo is used for temporary structures and agricultural huts.

Alang-alang (*Imperata cylindrica*) grass, with its tall rigid stems, is ideal for thatching. It is very common, growing in the forest and by water. It also appears on cleared and abandoned ground. Related to sugar cane, it belongs to the *Andropogon* family. *Alang-alang* has a subterranean creeping stem, which means it can survive fire when other grasses disappear. It is easy to gather, and stiff bundles are tied either directly on to the roof purlins, or lashed or sewn onto bamboo battens for thatching.

Throughout the archipelago, it is the roof structure that is the dominant feature of traditional housing. Roofs are always steeply pitched to ensure that the rain runs quickly off the thatch, although in many Indonesian houses the angle of the roof declines as it reaches the eaves so that the water is guided away from the foundations of the house.

Though zinc roofs have been growing in popularity since the turn of the century and now abound, most were of thatch or some kind of bamboo or wood shingle (ceramic tiles are only an alternative in Java and Bali). For most buildings, thatch is the only affordable alternative to zinc. Indonesian thatch comes from two different sources: from naturally occurring vegetation, and from by-products of agricultural crops. Plants are not specially cultivated for thatching as they are in some other parts of the world.

The thatch used depends on what is locally available. *Alang-alang* grass grows almost everywhere and is always a viable option. Rice straw is used in great rice-growing areas such as Bali. Over the rest of the archipelago palm leaf and other palm products are used. Palm leaves are harvested from wild trees or come from the plantations as by-products. Palm-leaf thatch is not very durable; some types can last as long as ten years, but most have to be replaced in less than three.

Palm-leaf thatch is generally made by splitting palm fronds and reinforcing the rib edge with a timber batten.

Thatch deteriorates through a combined process. Decay starts when the grasses or palm fronds are physically damaged, and the process is accelerated by exposure to sunlight. They are then prone to fungal attack in warm wet conditions, although the smoke from hearths has a preservative effect. To help preserve them, *nipa* or *rumbia* palm fronds are first soaked in water until they turn sour, then dried and preferably cured over a fire before the thatch is laid. The aim of the thatcher is to expose the barest minimum of thatching material to the weather. To achieve this, the roofs must be steeply pitched and the thatch tightly packed so that the rain runs over the surface, rather than penetrating the material. If the thatching is skilfully done and the material relatively durable, it will, inevitably, erode with the passage of time, but will still remain resistant to the elements. The durability of palm-leaf thatch will depend on its thickness and the care with which it is laid.

Thatch has its disadvantages. It can only be used to cover steeply pitched roofs that are either conical or have a central ridge, and thatching makes roof intersections or valleys impossible. It is vulnerable to fire and harbours insects and rodents, which in turn attract snakes.

Thatching with grass, like tiling, involves placing the material in ascending and overlapping courses to cover the roof surface so that rain flows down to the ground as quickly as possible. Bundles of grass are either tied directly onto the purlins or are first bound or sewn to a batten. Once the entire surface of the roof is covered, a ridge roll or ridge rolls of bound grass laid along the ridge pole maintains the steep pitch of the top two courses of thatch. The ridge must then be sealed, with another layer of grass or palm leaf, with a wooden cover or even with a piece of zinc roofing.

The techniques for thatching with palm leaf vary according to the type of leaf. Feathery leaves such as those of the coconut palm are composed of leaflets attached to both sides of a linear stem. The leaves are cut from the tree when mature, and dried in the sun. The central rib is then split to form two shingles. Alternatively, all the leaflets may be bent to one side of the rib and plaited together to form a single, strong thatch panel. If the leaflets are attached to the central rib at a sharp angle, they will be cut off and formed into shingles. Detached segments of the *nipa* palm are folded down one quarter of their length so that they overlap a bamboo batten, and then sewn firmly down. The palm-leaf panels are attached to the roof from the bottom up. No battens are needed. The thicker the thatch, which depends on how closely the panels are spaced, the more durable it will be. Care must be taken to avoid placing the panels too closely together, otherwise they will lie too flat, even though the roof is sloping, and water will penetrate the thatch rather than running off. Fan-shaped palm leaves must be dried

A batten of thatch, made of a split interwoven coconut leaf.

and flattened before they are ready for use. They are tied to the roof purlins so that they overlap.

The major problem with palm thatch is that, unlike grass, it is difficult to make a watertight gable, because at each end of the roof the tip of each rib will be exposed and likely to direct water back into the thatch. Palm leaves are traditionally used only on full-hipped roofs where the eave-line is continuous and unbroken around all four sides of the building; even here, however, the thatcher must ensure that the thatch is weathertight along the four hip rafters. The ridge of palm-leaf thatched roofs is achieved either by bending leaves over the apex of the ridge and tying or stitching them down, or covering them with wood or a metal sheet.

The use of ceramic tiles for roofing is restricted to Bali and Java. Flat, rectangular tiles have been used since the fourteenth century, and are still found today, but more common now are the tiles with an 'S'-shaped cross-section which, when they overlap each other, combine the functions of both conduit and joint cover. Tongue-shaped shingles of ironwood or teak are used on important public buildings in urban centres, particularly in Java and Bali.

All over Indonesia half rounds of bamboo with their inner diaphragms removed are used in the manner of Roman tiles, laid out, open face up, perpendicular to the roof purlins. Half rounds are then placed face down over them to link them all into an integrated system that both channels rainwater away and seals the roof. Their use is restricted to less important buildings and temporary structures. Sections of whole bamboo culms are used in an ingenious manner to roof over the *tongkonan* – the Toraja houses of origin. They form an extremely long-lasting roof structure. When Tana Toraja villagers use zinc instead of bamboo, however, they do not have to sacrifice so many pigs, and therefore save themselves a great deal of money.

Zinc roofs, which have in many cases replaced the old thatched roofs, are high thermal conductors with low insulation properties. They have some advantages over thatch as in many cases they are now cheaper to buy, easier to install, require no maintenance and do not constantly flake. On the other hand, they rust quickly, trap heat in hot weather and are so noisy when it rains that they drown all conversation.

In most parts of the archipelago, zinc roofs are used very skilfully, only covering those areas of the house that are not used during the daytime, where the intense heat would make conditions unbearable (although the shade from coconut trees planted nearby can help immensely). Such are their conductive properties, however, that at night they cool down extremely rapidly, a change in temperature that is felt acutely in the tropical regions, with their relatively even temperatures.

Indonesian villagers build their own houses with the aid of their neighbours and sometimes a carpenter or master builder. Apart from these specialists, no one gets paid, as there is little ready money in these societies. The workers are fed while the building is in progress and expect their help to be reciprocated when they in turn come to construct a new house, or to repair an old one. When major, consciously ostentatious houses are built by aristocrats in such places as Nias, Tana Toraja and the Batak lands, the workers are rewarded with a great feast on completion or occupation of the building, entailing the ritual slaughter of pigs and buffalo. The giving of such feasts bestows upon these aristocratic house builders a status akin to that of living gods. The beams of the chief's house at Bawomataluo in Nias are lined with the jaw bones of pigs eaten at such a feast.

Certain conventions are observed in house-building all over the archipelago. The spirits of trees are respected, and in many areas it is traditional to make offerings to a tree before it is felled. Timber is always incorporated into a structure in the direction the wood grew – to plant a timber pole upside-down would be unthinkable, as this is believed to bring misfortune.

In the Malay world, a *bomoh*, a spirit medium, is employed 'to search for the base of the house'. Much influenced by the principles of Chinese geomancy, the *bomoh* searches out an auspicious site for the house and recites incantations that ensure the passage of spirits will not disturb the peace of the occupants. Once this is accomplished, the structural components of the house are laid out on the ground and then the holes for the piles are dug. The vertical parts of the house are first laid out in the predetermined direction.

A panel of painted interwoven split bamboo decorating the gable of a Simalungun Batak rumah adat, *north Sumatra.*

In Bali, the pillars of the house must be erected in a certain order, always starting in the north-east corner and continuing in a clockwise direction. The pillars of a Malay house are usually obtained from a single tree trunk, and must be distributed around the house in the location in which the wood grew – for example, the central part of the trunk will form the central pillar, the western segment the middle pillar to the west, the north-west segment the north-west corner pillar. Pillars are raised by means of ropes, and then stabilizing beams are slotted and then wedged into them in pre-mortised holes.

When the beamwork of the house is finished, but before the roof is covered, various ceremonies take place. In Java a bunch of flowers and a coconut are tied to one end of the ridge, and pieces of red, black and white cloth are placed between the pillars and the beams. In east and central Java a nail engraved with sacred Arabic calligraphy is solemnly driven into the ridge beam. In the Balinese parts of Lombok, three freshly cut sugar canes are placed erect on top of the ridge beam.

Buildings are assembled without nails. Mortises are made bigger than the tenons that are to be fitted into them, secured by hammering in wedges, or pegs. Frame members are very often simply lashed together with extremely tough rattan or *ijuk* cord. This form of construction has two distinct advantages: it can be easily dismantled and reassembled at a new location, and is better able to withstand earthquakes.

Tools are simple hammers, chisels, saws, axes and adzes and nowadays a plane for preparing planking. Machetes of all shapes and sizes are used constantly for cutting and trimming bindings and thatching materials.

The piles of a traditional house support a great ring beam, but in many cases they also run straight up to take the weight of the roof directly. Walls are generally non-loadbearing, and are therefore not vital structural elements. They are usually made up of prefabricated screens attached to the main structure of posts and beams, which carries the load of the roof and in many cases the floor as well. Walls are of planking, interwoven split bamboo or woven palm leaf. Loadbearing walls of Javanese and Balinese ground-built dwellings are of brick, tuff or other masonry.

Corner section of a sopo (a Toba Batak *rice barn), showing the* labe-labe, *the longitudinal beam. A wooden disc is positioned on top of the corner post to stop rodents from getting into the granary. Cross-beams are mortised into the substructure both to stabilize it and to provide a night-time stall for animals.*

The Malay house is taken as a model for most of the housing in many of the humid coastal regions of the archipelago. Made of timber and raised on stilts, it has a post-and-lintel structure with wooden or bamboo walls and a thatched roof. Windows are plentiful, providing good ventilation and excellent views. It is cool and pleasant to live in, with large open, interior spaces and few partitions. It is cheap to build and easy to extend or dismantle.

Many traditional Indonesian houses are left unadorned, relying for their undoubted beauty upon the natural colouring of the woods and thatching materials. The Batak, Minangkabau and Toraja, however, decorate their buildings with bas-relief carved wooden panels and painting, and carved finials and other ornaments can be found on houses throughout the islands. Complex terracotta finials crown nearly all traditional Balinese buildings, which are often also decorated with very fine wood and stone carving.

Traditional Indonesian architecture has always had an almost symbiotic relationship with its surrounding environment. Built with materials collected from the fields and forests, and very simple tools, the houses, granaries and public buildings consequently blend harmoniously with their natural habitat. Inevitably, overexploitation of the forests has meant that many varieties of superb timber are no longer to be had, and modern twentieth-century materials are now available to those that can afford them; but housing traditions in any case never remain static for very long. The Toraja houses of origin, for example, have changed gradually over the years, as one element has been accentuated, another diminished, whilst they still retain their basic form. As long as the various regions of Indonesia preserve their cultural differences, and trees continue to grow in the surrounding countryside, Indonesians will make beautiful houses fully adapted to the local climate and ecology, with an unstinting use of their own labour and careful expenditure of their own financial resources.

2
Sumatra
Island of Gold

SUMATRA is the fourth largest island in the world, known as the 'island of gold' from the times of Marco Polo. With its tea, pepper and rubber plantations, its oil and tin, and other mineral resources, it is the richest part of Indonesia, and home to the most diverse range of people in the whole archipelago. From historic Aceh at its northern tip down the eastern coast to Pekanbaru, Jambi and Palembang live people of predominantly Malay origin. In the highlands of the northern part of the island dwell the Batak tribes, who farm the beautiful fertile valleys around great, still Lake Toba. The lush west of central Sumatra is home to the sophisticated matrilineal Minangkabau and to the south, neighbouring Java, are the pepper-rich lands of Lampung. Along the west coast lies a string of islands, the most notable of which are Nias and the Mentawai group.

Sumatra, which is neatly bisected by the equator, has a monsoon climate, with a wet season that differs somewhat between the northern and southern parts of the island but generally lasts from October until May. There is, however, no extended rainless period that could be called a dry season. Despite large-scale timber extraction, there are still millions of acres of unexploited rain forest which provide building materials, though the availability of the great hardwood trees that allowed construction on the magnificent scale of the past is now strictly limited. Architecturally, Sumatra is as diverse as its population, but wooden houses, raised on piles and built of locally gathered materials, with steeply pitched, thatched or zinc roofs, are most common.

The most culturally cosmopolitan areas of Sumatra are the former princedoms that stretch down the eastern seaboard from Aceh to Palembang; situated along the great Malacca Straits trading route, they were constantly exposed to fresh political, economic, cultural and religious influences. Aceh, the northernmost sultanate, was always the most prominent politically. Allied in turn to both the Turkish and the Mughal empires and converted to Islam at the end of the thirteenth century, Aceh remained fiercely independent until the end of the nineteenth century when its alliance with the British, first sought after in the days of Elizabeth I in the sixteenth century, lapsed, and Dutch colonizers took over in a war of conquest that was to last nearly forty years.

The Acehnese style of building has much in common with that of the Malayan peninsula across the water; indeed, there has been an extremely long history of cross-migration and intermarriage across the Straits of Malacca. The most striking features of Acehnese houses are their beautiful gables of carved and fretted wood, which are known as *tolak angin* ('shield against the wind'). These incline slightly outwards at an angle of about thirty degrees from the vertical, in the same manner as the ancient Dong-Son model. The houses conform to the basic Malay floor plan with only a few variations. As with the Malay house, the floors of different quarters are at different levels; the most prestigious is the bedroom, which occupies the centre of the house and is at the highest level. A triangular attic space is created by laying a ceiling over the living quarters to form a storage area for valuables. Fronting onto the street, at a lower level than the central portion of the house, is the verandah that forms the men's part of the building, and this is also the public area for receiving guests. Parallel to this, flanking the other side of the bedroom area, is another verandah virtually identical in plan and elevation, which is the women's domain. This rear verandah leads off to a kitchen at yet a lower level. The houses are usually oriented north or south on either side of a road running east to west. The gables face east and west on an axis that was probably originally meant to catch the prevailing winds, and later received the religious sanction of Islam (as Mecca lies to the west). The houses are built on pillars and catch the upper breezes, and the intricate tracery of stylized floral forms and repeated spirals that pierce the gables helps to draw in the cooling air and expel the heat that collects inside. The windows increase ventilation, and are also decorated, as are the outer skirting around the base of the walls, the doors, the inner dividing panels, roof beams and staircases. Floors are of wooden planking or rattan, and walls are generally of wood, but sometimes interwoven split bamboo or woven coconut leaves are used. Roofs can be thatched with sago or *nipa* palm leaves, but are now mostly zinc.

Construction techniques are similar to those in other parts of the archipelago: sugar-palm twine commonly serves as lashing and wooden pegs and wedges are used instead of nails and screws (the pegs are small, and must be locked in by means of the wedges). This custom, widespread over the archipelago, enables the house to be dismantled and transported to another location, which often happens upon the death of the owner; the inheritors may even split the house up between them. (Although Aceh society has strong patriarchal Islamic traits, the Acehnese house owner is most likely to be a woman. Marriage in Aceh is matrilocal. When a daughter marries, her father gives her a separate dwelling; if he cannot afford that, he will erect an annexe for her to one side of the house.)

Gajo is an isolated inland district of Sumatra bordering on Aceh. The Gajo *rumah adat* is known as an *uma*. It is a pile-built communal dwelling inhabited by a number of related families, longer than the typical Aceh house but similar in layout, and as in Aceh consists of a men's front gallery, central sleeping quarters and rear women's gallery.

Influenced by the Acehnese style, and seemingly oblivious to and unaffected by the nearby Minangkabau, are the houses found in the western part of Siberut

Island in the Mentawai group. These, however, are built on a much larger scale, and were formerly used as *uma* longhouses by the Sakuddei tribe. The Sakuddei were forced to abandon their traditional way of life through government intervention in the 1950s and 1960s, but since then some attempt has been made to re-establish them in their former areas of settlement.

Uma longhouses are rectangular with a verandah at each end and can be as large as 300 square metres (975 sq. ft) in area. They are pile-built, and traditionally they have no windows. Inside they are separated into different dwelling spaces with crossways partitions, which usually have interconnecting doors. Villages are built near river banks and consist of one or more *uma* communal house surrounded by single-storey family houses known as *lalep*. These villages can be quite sizeable, housing up to several hundred people. Large villages are divided into sections, each occupied by patrilineal clans made up of a group of families with its own *uma*. Widows and bachelors in the community have their own dwellings known as *rusuk,* which are of the same design as the family longhouse except that they have no altar. Mentawai society is essentially egalitarian. The *uma* is the focus of social, religious and political life and it is here that everyone – women and children included – takes part in the meetings called to discuss matters affecting the community. Like many Indonesians, the Mentawaians believe in a separable soul that leaves the body at death to become a ghost. To protect themselves from these spirits, fetish sticks are placed by the entrances in the log wall that both surrounds and fortifies the village and forms a stockade for cattle.

Enggano is a group of islands to the west of Bengkulu. Isolated from the cultural mainstream, the inhabitants were still using stone axes in 1770 when European expeditions reached the islands. Villages consist of groups of round houses about 9 metres (30 ft) in diameter raised on ironwood pillars. Walls are of wood or bamboo, roofs thatched with woven rattan leaves. A notched wooden beam affords access to the house, which in fact is one large room surrounding a hearth. This is where the adults sleep; the children and adolescents sleep in less carefully built rooms and shelters. Each village has a rectangular pile-built meeting hall known as *kadiofe* which, under its rattan roof, is open on all four sides.

Moving a long way south from Aceh along the eastern seaboard, one comes to the old principality of Jambi. Formerly a great trading port and centre for batik production, it had long been a focus of Dutch influence, and is famous for its pepper exports. Houses here, like those in Aceh, are pile-built and oriented north and south, with the rooms at different levels. The kitchen is external. Their most outstanding decorative features are their beautifully carved and painted pediments that adorn the gables of the main buildings, with their delicately intertwined floral motifs in bas-relief. The eaves are often embellished with a fretted wooden pelmet. The main entrance to the house is reached by means of an often imposing stairway wth carved wood or cast-iron balustrades. Jambi houses can be of great size, frequently up to 200 square metres (650 sq. ft) in area.

Palembang is the great city of southern Sumatra. It is the centre of the oil industry, so vital to Sumatran and Indonesian wealth. Traditional Palembang houses are known as *rumah lima*, and are built in the Malay style similarly to those of Jambi. The Palembang region is crossed by great tidal rivers. On the banks of the River Musi, houses are set on piles that are often as tall as 5 metres (16 ft), to withstand the extremely strong tidal flooding. The course of the river determines the orientation of the house, as the facade always fronts onto the river. There is no rear verandah and access to the kitchen, which is set on lower piles at the rear of the house, is from the outside only.

Lampung is the rugged, sparsely populated, southern part of the island bordering on the Sunda Strait and Java. The Lampungese are descended from the 'ancient people' (possibly the Bataks) and the Sundanese of west Java. For centuries it was a tributary to Banten, across the Sunda Strait. Lampung and neighbouring Bengkulu were the world's foremost source of pepper, and with the riches generated from this trade a stratified society developed that was inclined to the ostentatious display of fine ritual textiles and the building of beautiful houses.

A painted motif on a rattan screen from Lampung.

Lampung *rumah adat*, known as *nua*, are constructed of wood on 1.8 metre (6 ft) piles, following the Malay model. The front of the house incorporates a balcony and the eaves are decorated with pierced wooden fretwork rather in the manner of Acehnese houses. The villages are located by rivers and surrounded by fences safeguarding poultry, firewood and other possessions. The houses may be one or two storeys high, and are built of wood, or part wood and part bamboo or bark. They have a square, pyramid-shaped roof, which at first descends steeply from its apex (which is crowned with a decorative sphere) and then sweeps down to the eaves at a greatly reduced pitch. The shallower slope covers a verandah that runs all the way round the house.

The *nua* are grouped around the *sesat*, the communal house. The *sesat* is found in the oldest part of each village, where the influence of Islam is least felt. It is usually built on piles and consists of one room with a number of subdivisions, which serve to segregate people of different class. Its walls and floor are of bamboo.

Rumah adat in Bengkulu are square and built to the Malay plan. Raised on square wooden piles about 2.5 metres (8 ft) high, they have a central staircase leading up to the front of the house. The overhanging eaves of the roof cover verandahs at the front and back that have balustrades embellished with wooden fretwork. The hipped roof, which increases in slope half way up, is covered with ceramic tiles or wooden shingles. As with all Malay-style houses, there is an abundance of windows, often louvred to cope with the humid climate.

The Bataks are a large ethnic group who farm the fertile valleys in the highlands of north-central Sumatra. They are renowned both for their spirit of independence and their craftsmanship in metal, textiles and wood. Their culture centres around the great still Lake Toba and the sacred island of Samosir that lies within it. The Bataks are divided into six groups who speak different but related languages: the Angkola and the Mandailing to the south, who were Islamicized during the murderous internecine Padri wars from 1820 to 1837, the Toba who were converted to Christianity by Protestant German missionaries from 1864 onwards, and to the north the Pakpak/Diari, the Simalungun and the Karo who are now mostly Christian (though some are Muslim). Elements of the ancient Batak religion linger on, however, particularly among the Karo.

The Batak build some of the most dramatic traditional houses in the archipelago. The boat-shaped houses of the Toba, with their magnificently carved gables and upsweeping roof ridges, and those of the Karo, which rise up in fantastic tiers, are both built on piles and derive from an ancient Dong-Son model.

There is a great deal of variety in the architecture of the houses and the layout of the villages of the six Batak groups. The Toba and Karo Batak inhabit permanent villages and exist on irrigated rice and vegetable cultivation. The traditional slash-and-burn agricultural practice of the Angkola, the Mandailing and the Pakpak, however, demanded frequent change of land and long fallow periods; consequently their villages were only semi-permanent.

The cultivation of irrigated rice can support a large population, so the Toba and the Karo live in villages that are often clustered quite close together. The size of each village, however, is restricted to about ten dwellings, to avoid taking up too much of the land. In those areas still dependent on unirrigated, slash-and-burn agricultural production, smaller villages containing only a handful of houses are the norm. Regardless of size, villages are always located as near as possible to the fields and to the all-important water course. Before the twentieth century, the Batak country was prone to internecine wars; consequently, villages were also often sited in an easily defensible position. Pakpak villages were strongly fortified with a high bamboo stockade, Toba villages with an impenetrable barrier of earthen ramparts set with bamboo fencing and planted with trees.

Each of the different Batak groups lays out its village according to its own rules and traditions. Toba Batak houses stand side by side with their front gables facing the village street and, customarily, the rice granary belonging to each house would stand opposite it as part of a complementary row on the other side (although many have now been demolished). The street between the rice granaries and the houses is known as the *alaman* and is used as a work area and a place for drying rice. The Mandailing also build their houses along a village street, but with the front gable facing the adjoining house's back gable in the manner of the neighbouring Minangkabau. In Karo villages the houses are not laid out in streets but are clustered around the focal point of the village where the meeting hall (*bale*) and the rice pounding house (*lesung*) are situated. Pakpak villages are similar in layout to those of the Karo.

There are three main types of building that are common to all the different Batak groups, the *bale*, the *rumah* (house) and the *sopo* (rice barn). Traditionally the *rumah* was a large house in which a group of families would live communally. The interior living space was shared during the day and only divided up at night for family privacy by means of cloth or matting drapes.

Carving adorning the facade of a Batak house.

Carved and painted lizard motif from a Karo Batak rice barn and (far right) *a* singa *motif from a Toba Batak gable.*

The *rumah adat* of the Toba Batak is known as a *jabu* in the Toba language, and is made up of three sections. Its substructure consists of large wooden pillars that rest on flat stones (or nowadays concrete plinths) to protect them from rot caused by rising damp. Some of these pillars support longitudinal beams known as *labe-labe*, which run along the length of the house at head height to carry the massive roof; others bear the weight of two huge beams with carved *singa* heads which, with two lateral beams mortised into them, form a great ring beam supporting the rather cramped living space. The substructure is made stronger by mortising a system of beams into the piles, which also creates night-time stalls for cattle. The walls are of light construction and lean outwards, giving added stability to the whole structure. The top of the wall and the wall-plate that supports the rafters are hung from the *labe-labe* with rattan cords. The bottom of the wall rests on the ring-beam. The rafters spring from the wall plate and are angled outwards to produce the curve of the roof. There are no horizontal battens for bracing, but reinforcement is supplied by diagonal ties running from the middle of the *labe-labe* to the tips of the gable-ends.

The gigantic roof, traditionally covered in thatch, dominates the whole building. As there are no internal roof trusses, a large interior space remains. The roof is steeply pitched and saddleback-shaped, with sharply projecting triangular gables and eaves that overlap the substructure all the way round the house. The front gable extends much further out than the rear gable and is richly decorated with carved and painted motifs of suns, stars, cockerels and geometric motifs in

red, white and black. The rear gable is left plain. The living area, which is supported by two pairs of finely carved lateral and transverse beams, is in fact rather cramped, smoky from the fire in the central hearth, and dark. Light is only admitted through small windows, one set into each of the side and rear walls, but this is of little consequence as this area is mainly used to sleep in, with most of the inhabitants' time spent outdoors. A flat wooden ceiling roofs over the front third of the living area to form an attic space above, where the sacred family heirlooms and sometimes the family shrine are stored. Access to this space is provided by a tree-trunk ladder. The Toba used to cook over a hearth at the front of the living room, but now, with improved standards of hygiene, the kitchen is often situated in an extension at the back of the house.

Above, left *A Toba Batak rice barn and* (below) *a Toba Batak house.*

Above *A Karo Batak house.*

Opposite *Section of a Karo Batak house.*

Communal houses have become rare amongst the Toba Batak. Houses are now built in the Malay style using a combination of modern and traditional materials. These are roomier, airier, let in more light and are usually cheaper to build, but they are not as prestigious as the *jabu*. For those Toba still living in the traditional manner, smaller single-family dwellings are now the norm. Although they conform to the design of the *jabu*, access is no longer through a trap door concealing interior steps, but by wooden stairs leading up to a door in the front wall of the house: an innovation which, whilst obviously more convenient, is also a reflection of less dangerous times.

Many people now live in converted rice barns, which are easily adapted by walling off the open-air section that lies between the substructure and the roof and putting a door in the front. Built in a similar style and manner to the *jabu*, rice barns are now very rarely used for their original purpose. Rice was stored within the roof, the weight of which was supported on six great wooden pillars which have large wooden discs at the top to prevent rodents from crawling up into the storage space. The open platform beneath the roof was used as a working and general recreational area and as a sleeping place for guests and unmarried men.

Of all the Bataks, the Karo were the most resistant to outside influences and adhered most strongly to their native religion. They had the most complex and

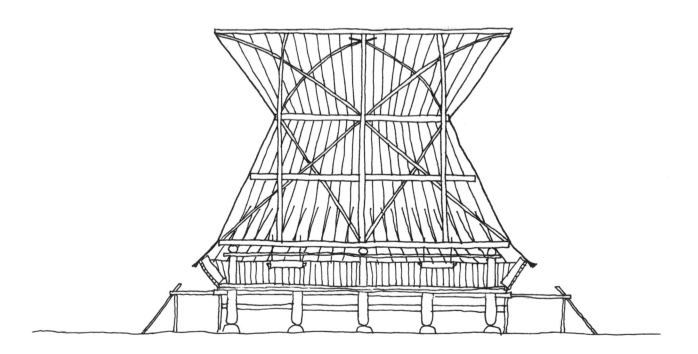

varied of architectural styles, the greatest range of traditional buildings and a huge diversity of forms in which these buildings could be constructed. Houses, meeting halls, rice barns, rice threshing houses and ossuaries were the traditional structures built by the Karo, but sadly they have mainly fallen into disuse and decay. These buildings are set onto a substructure assembled either with pillars driven straight into the ground and cross-braced just below the level of the house floor (a *rumah pasuk*), or in the probably more ancient manner whereby trimmed poles are laid horizontally on top of each other in a rectangular grid, with the lateral and longitudinal poles set into each other (a *rumah sangka manuk*). With this version, the substructure rests on stone blocks, and the cornerposts of the house are set into holes bored in the ends of the interlocking cross beams, stabilizing the whole frame. There is yet another form of substructure, which resembles Toba Batak architecture. With this version, the upright wooden pillars rest on flat stones and are thereby protected from rot. They have cross beams set into them midway between the ground and the floor level, giving added stability and creating an enclosure under the house that can be used as a stall for livestock.

Even more varied are the Karo Batak roof forms, but they can be divided into two basic types. One is supported by an almost square substructure from which the roof rises up in a uniform manner to form a roughly symmetrical pyramid. The other is a hipped gabled roof whose narrow ends slope down below the projecting gable. These can be made more decorative by building on a contrasting upper part, and in the case of the palaces of the rajas, yet another miniature building can be set above this. Karo Batak gables are decorated with panels of interwoven split bamboo painted in contrasting colours. The profile of a Karo house zig-zagging up to the sky is supposed to represent an animist in the posture of prayer.

A long beam divides the living quarters of the Karo house into two. There are four hearths, two on each side of the beam, each used by one or two families. The whole house can support up to eight families. There are no interior partitions, though mats and cloths draped around each family's separate sleeping quarters at night ensure a certain degree of privacy. Although a Toba communal house is lived in by members of an extended family, that of the Karo can be occupied by families that may not be directly related. The long horizontal beams that frame the living area are giant tree trunks whose bases must always meet in the corner occupied by the master of the house. According to the complicated cosmology of the Karo the corner opposite this must always face east. One entrance to the house has wooden handles on either side and a large wooden step or 'seat'. By leaning back into the house, whilst gripping the handles, women used to give birth onto the springy bamboo floor. They were sheltered from the public gaze by a palm-leaf screen.

Opposite 1 *The* singa *is a mythical, dragon-like creature, and is central to Batak art. It has an apotropaic function, and here adorns a contemporary public meeting hall at Tarutung, in the lands of the Toba Batak in northern Sumatra.*

Lake Toba, deep and still, is the sacred centre of Sumatra's Batak lands. On the large island of Samosir, thrust up into the middle of the lake by prehistoric volcanic activity, and on the lakeside shore, the most magnificent ancestral homes of the Toba Batak can be found. They are raised on pillars, with steeply pitched saddleback roofs, and have carved and painted walls. **2** A house set on wooden pillars, thatched with ijuk *(sugar-palm fibre)*, in Tomok village, Samosir Island. **3** The doorway and window of a sopo *(rice barn)* that has in recent years been converted into a house, in Tomok village. **4** A singa *head* bordered with carved and painted floral panels adorning the front of a house in Simanindo village, at Samosir's northern tip. **5** A woman weaving an ulos *(cloth)* in the shelter of the undercroft of an old sopo in Ambarita village, Samosir.

3△   4△

5△

7 △

Traditional Toba Batak houses are known for their upsweeping roof ridges and elaborate decoration. 6 A contemporary single-family house on Samosir Island. It has a zinc roof, a storage gallery and carved and painted gables. 7 A traditional house by the still waters of Lake Toba.
8 A house and barn thatched with ijuk.
9 Rice storage jars are kept in the gallery of a house near Ambarita village. 10 The wall of a house is decorated with a singa head, two pairs of carved breasts (which will be balanced by male symbols on another part of the building), a heavily stylized singa head within a carved and painted disc, and horizontal carved and painted bands of floral and vegetal motifs.

◁ 6

8 △

9 △

10 △

11 △

11 The Toba Batak people have a hierarchical, patriarchal society, that accords much reverence to the dead. The graves of their kings are marked with great carved stone monoliths and set in sacred groves. This king's sarcophagus and surrounding graves lie in the sacred grove at Tomok village, Samosir Island. 12 The rafters and purlins of a Toba roof thatched with ijuk. Although ijuk is a long-lasting form of thatch, zinc roofs are now rather commonplace. 13 A roof support beam and pegging, part of a Toba house in a Simanindo village, Samosir. 14 The gallery of a house in Tomok village. The ventilation ducts are built into the gable, and the cross brace is decorated with a singa head.

12 △

13 △

14 ▷

Of all the Batak tribes, the Karo have been least affected by modernizing influences, and they retain deeply held faith in their indigenous religion. They have developed the most varied of architectural styles and the greatest range of traditional buildings in Indonesia. Houses, meeting halls, ossuaries, rice barns and threshing houses are built on substructures that are either supported on pillars planted straight into the ground or made of trimmed poles laid horizontally in a rectangular grid, in the manner of a log cabin. **15** A communal house, with a hipped gabled roof crowned with buffalo-horn finials. The gables are decorated with painted interwoven split bamboo. The massive ring beam, which is supported on wooden pillars, is painted and carved with floral and vegetal motifs. Attached to the walls are woven images of elongated lizards, symbols of male power. **16** A bridal couple standing on the ture-ture, *the bamboo platform outside their house in Lingga village.*

16 △

◁**15**

49

17 △

18 △

19 △

Buildings of the Karo Batak are complex and often elaborately decorated. The design of the houses in the Karo village of Lingga has remained unchanged for centuries, and many are supposed to be over 250 years old. They were built entirely without nails. **17** An ornate facade and gable. **18** A meeting house for young bachelors. The roof structure – two crossed gabled roofs surmounting the basic pyramid shape – is typical of the Karo. It is thatched with ijuk and the gables are decorated with painted interwoven split bamboo. The sheltered, unwalled space is used by the young men as a recreational area. **19** The wooden piles that support this house have cross beams mortised into them to form a night-time corral for cattle. Ferns grow out of the thatch. **20** The platform of the bachelors' meeting house. **21** Pairs of woven elongated lizards adorn the walls and two male figures are painted onto a split bamboo gable.

20 △

21 ▷

22△

23△

The Simalungun Bataks are to be found
north-east of Lake Toba. Their
architectural forms are akin to those of the
Toba, but they are also influenced by Karo
building. **22** Two houses that form part of
the royal palace complex in Pematang
Purba. One is raised on beautifully painted
and carved wooden pillars, and interwoven
split bamboo, painted in contrasting black-
and-white, decorates the gable ends. The
other house frame is supported on
horizontal beams notched into each other.
23 A lesung (rice-pounding barn) in
Pematang Purba. Painted wooden pillars
support the roof structure (**24**).

24 ▷

25 △

Northern Sumatra still has vast areas of rain forest, an abundant source of timber, put to use with immense skill by the Bataks. **25** The floor supports, pillars and split bamboo walls of a house in Pematang Purba. **26** Stripped tree trunks, notched and laid horizontally, form a log-cabin style foundation to a house in the Pematang Purba royal complex. **27** The facade of the public meeting hall at Tarutung, built in the traditional Toba Batak style with finely painted and carved cross-beam supports surmounted by a singa *finial*. **28** A pair of roof finials in the shape of buffalo heads are made with ijuk fibre, but are crowned with real buffalo horns. The roof is thatched with ijuk.

26 ▽

27 △

30 △

The Minangkabau once ruled over most of central Sumatra, but were pressed back into the western highlands in the fourteenth century, with the coming of Islam. Although the Minangkabau are now Muslim, certain aspects of their old culture survive. Their society remains matrilineal, and the women are the property owners and head the household. The men, on the other hand, travel abroad on business – a custom known as merantau – and the revenue from these trips contributes to the funding of traditional-style building.
29 An old rumah gadang (the Minangkabau term for traditional house), in Bukittinggi, now used as a museum. The gracefully upswept multiple gables and the profusely carved and painted front and side walls are typical of Minangkabau architecture. 30 The gable of a contemporary public building in Bukittinggi. Roof forms derived from traditional Minangkabau architecture are often added to modern, reinforced concrete buildings in an effort to strengthen cultural links with the past.

31 A Minangkabau mosque and madrassah set amidst the padi fields of west Sumatra. The Malay-style multi-tiered roof contrasts with the more usual Islamic onion-shaped domes. **32** The main street of a highland Minangkabau village near Pagarruyung, from which an array of upswept gables can be seen. The walls of the house in the foreground are of crudely interwoven split bamboo. **33** The front elevation of the rebuilt royal palace at Pagarruyung. The palace, now a museum, has a tiered roof; the ruler used to practise white magic in its uppermost part. **34** The edges of the eaves, the ridges and the finials on the palace roof at Pagarruyung are all created by combining ijuk fibre with decorative metal bindings (35).

32 △

◁31

33 ∧

34 △

35 △

36 △

37 △

Many consider Minangkabau architecture, with its tiered gables and gracefully upsweeping ridge ends, to be the most beautiful form of traditional housing in the whole of Indonesia. Walls are set with shuttered windows and incised with profuse floral carving. **36** A rice barn within the royal palace complex at Pagarruyung. **37** The walls of the royal palace at Pagarruyung are painted and carved, and decorative beading covers the supporting wooden piles. The inner faces of the shutters are also decorated, as they will be visible from the outside when the shutters are open. **38** The floral carving on the wall panels is painted in the Minangkabau colours thought to have been derived from Chinese brocades. **39** The boys' circumcision hall seen from the room of magic at the top of the sultan's palace at Pagarruyung.

38 △

Riau is made up of four mainland districts and more than three thousand largely uninhabited islands that lie off the eastern coast of Sumatra. Its predominantly Malay inhabitants build houses known as rumah lipat kijang, *a name that alludes to the hairpin-shape of their roofs. The houses are built on pillars with a shaded porch set into the front or side, and adorned with carvings of birds, bees and flowers.*
40 *A barred window with louvred shutters bordered by carved wooden panelling top and bottom.* **41** *Crossed wooden finials carved with floral motifs, surmounting a roof covered with teak shingles.* **42** *One side of a curved double staircase that leads up to an extended verandah serving as a reception area. The staircase is of cement and tiles, and the ornamental slatted balustrades and roof flashing are of wood.*

41 △

◁40

Bawomataluo, a large village in southern Nias, is renowned for its vernacular architecture, the main feature of which is its monumental chief's house, the omo sebua. **43** The omo sebua and 'jumping stone', once used as a mock-stockade by young men training for inter-village raids. The flat megaliths in front of the house were used to display bodies. **44** The view of Orihili village from Bawomataluo. **45** A terrace of commoners' houses, carried on ironwood pillars supported by diagonal trusses. A woman stands in the ventilation flap of a house; this flap is likened to a curl on top of a child's head. **46** The village founder's stone megalith, carved with human figures and a shark. A stone phallus can be seen in the background. **47** The balconies of the houses are said to derive their shape from the stern ends of Dutch galleons. **48** Massive vertical and diagonal ironwood pillars support the omo sebua, in front of which carved stone seats in the shape of treasure chests can be seen. Overleaf **49** The omo sebua looks out over the terraces of commoners' houses lining the paved street.

44 △

◁43

45 △

46 △

47 △

48 △

51 △

The interior of the omo sebua at
Bawomataluo is adorned with hardwood –
often ebony – carvings. Ebony is extremely
rare elsewhere in the archipelago.
50 Carved ebony thrones in the main
room, which once held ancestor figures.
The thrones are shaded by carved palm-
leaf parasols, which are royal symbols. Jaw
bones of pigs slaughtered for the inaugural
feast are still displayed on racks all around
the room. **51** A central column carved out
of a single tree trunk forms the focus of the
main room, where carvings of monkeys are
hung from massive ironwood girders (**52**).
53 An ebony wall panel carved in bas-
relief, depicting a Dutch steamship
mounted with cannon, surrounded by
monkeys, a crocodile catching fish, and a
fish caught on a line. **54** An ebony panel
carved in bas-relief with images of the
chief's regalia – a comb, necklace, helmet
crest and the single earring that proclaims
masculinity.

◁50

52 △

53 △

54 △

Villages in southern Nias are built on strategic hilltops approached by steep stone stairways, and are laid out in one long street or to a cruciform plan. They are large (housing as many as five thousand people), which in former times made them easier to defend from slave-raiders. Not all building in south Nias is done on such a scale, however, and many buildings by the beach or in the fields are only temporary and lightweight. **55** A carved stone seat and megalith crown the steps that lead up to Bawomataluo from Orihili. **56** Fresh strips of palm-leaf, stitched into roofing panels. **57** Villagers constructing a shelter in the fields are about to thatch the roof with palm-leaf panels.

56 △

57 △

A Karo rice barn, known as a *sopo page*, is usually a rectangular building with a roof that is supported by four pillars on an open floor resting on a cross-beam structure similar to that of a log cabin. The roof is of cantilever construction with triangular gables, which are often beautifully decorated but have no weight-bearing function. Traditionally, the storage space within Karo granaries would have been shared between four families, but now they are rarely used for their original purpose.

The building most characteristic of the Karo is the skull-house or ossuary, known as a *geriten*. Built to a square ground plan, usually with a hipped, gabled roof, it can be constructed with cross beams or vertical pillars. *Geriten* were built by prestigious and wealthy families to store the skulls and larger bones of their dead. Poorer families would store the relics of their ancestors in the roof of their house above their own sleeping place.

The Karo and the other northern Bataks – the Simalungun and the Pakpak – traditionally built an open, roofed structure known as a *lesung*, set on pillars. Here the women met, to pound and dehusk rice in a series of depressions set in a great beam. The *lesung* also had social importance as a trysting place for adolescent boys and girls. The *lesung* have now fallen into disuse. Nowadays the northern Batak pound their rice in individual blocks of stone or wood set outside the family house, as the southern Batak have always done. It is increasingly common, however, to take rice to the rice mills which can be found in all the larger villages. Mandailing and Angkola *rumah adat* are now very rare, and surviving examples are simplified versions of the Toba style. Mandailing gables are topped with protective buffalo heads carved out of wood.

Throughout the Batak lands, people are abandoning their traditional forms of housing and building in the modern Indonesian style. The old social structure is no longer the force that it was. People are acquiring furniture and televisions, and there is no longer the space for them to live communally in the customary manner. The *rumah adat* is perceived as old-fashioned, and new building in the traditional Batak style will in future probably only be carried out for cultural reasons.

The Riau archipelago is made up of more than three thousand mainly uninhabited islands spread out over the large area of water that lies between Sumatra, Singapore and Borneo. The inhabitants are predominantly Malays. The traditional houses of Riau are known as *rumah lipat kijang*, a name that refers to the shape of the roof. The houses are set on four pillars and adorned with carvings of birds, bees and flowers. Building in the old style is currently undergoing something of a revival and, as is the growing trend all over Indonesia, older architectural elements are being incorporated into modern public buildings. Three different traditional styles of housing can be found in Riau. The first is the Malay style, raised on piles with either a single or double-tiered zinc roof, plenty of windows, each with pierced wood decoration above and below, and fretwork decorating the eaves and balustrades. Their most distinctive feature is a shaded porch that juts out from the centre of the house. A stone and tile double staircase leads up to the living level on either side of the porch. The undercroft is used to store the long Riau canoes.

The second type is also built to the Malay plan, on wooden piles but with a slightly concave saddleback roof. The roof, now almost invariably of zinc, projects out front and back over vertical gables. A staircase at the side affords access, and this is protected from the elements by an extension of the roof which slopes down to cover it. Decorative pierced wood panels with floral motifs protrude on either side of the front wall rather like the bowsprit of a ship. The windows here are also surrounded by beautiful pierced floral woodwork. Extra eaves at the front and back of the house project out over the windows to protect them from the driving monsoon rain. Entry to the kitchen at the rear of the house is by another unprotected stairway.

The third style of traditional house is rarely found today. With a great gabled roof tiled with wooden shingles and adorned with highly ornate, florally carved buffalo-horn finials, the great house itself is built to the Malay plan, raised on wooden piles. It has many louvred doors and windows and the projecting eaves shade a balcony that runs right around the house. An imposing stairway leads up to the entrance at the side.

The Minangkabau are a cultured, sophisticated ethnic group living in west Sumatra, and are one of the most economically successful peoples in Indonesia. Many are well educated, having benefited from the schools built by the colonial Dutch, who for many years had made Padang, the seaport of the Minangkabau country, an important administrative centre. Minangkabau territory was once a large kingdom that spread over most of central Sumatra and encompassed Jambi, Bengkulu and Palembang. With the coming of Islam in the fourteenth century, the Minangkabau were gradually pressed back and reduced to a collection of petty chiefdoms in the highlands of west Sumatra. The attempt in the early nineteenth century by both external and internal forces to impose orthodox Islam on all the Minangkabau was eventually defeated by the customary chiefs supported by the Dutch and the Bataks. This left Minangkabau society a curious hybrid within which the Islamic religion is observed but the culture remains matrilineal: descent and inheritance is traced through the female line. Women are the property owners; husbands are only tolerated in the house at certain times and under certain conditions, and have to return to their sisters' house to sleep.

Complementary to this is the Minangkabau custom of *merantau*, whereby many of the men will voyage as far afield as Malaysia, Java and even the Middle East, only returning to their villages at periodic intervals. The money earned on these business trips is remitted back to their home villages and is an important source of funding for the building of contemporary traditional housing.

Migration has sometimes been permanent: there has been a Minangkabau settlement in Negeri Sembilan (now in Malaysia) since the seventeenth century, and the chief of the Minangkabau is still also the ruler there. The Minangkabau of Negeri Sembilan have adopted the Malay-style roof construction, with a continuous ridge piece thatched with lengths of palm-leaf attached to battens. This structure is simpler, and has meant that the roof has lost its characteristic curve and now has blunter eaves, leaving it austere, yet still dignified and beautiful. Malay Islamic influence has dictated changes to the interior layout, and now women are more restricted to the rear of the house than is the case in Sumatra.

The Minangkabau *rumah adat,* with its multiple gables and upsweeping ridge ends, is probably the most beautiful form of housing in the whole Indonesian archipelago. In contrast to the houses of the Toba Batak, where the roof essentially creates the living area, the roof of a Minangkabau house rests gracefully on top. Walls are of much greater importance; the front and side walls are set with shuttered windows and incised with beautiful and profuse floral carving. Colours are mainly red and white (favoured by the Chinese), and the carved motifs are the same as those to be found on the glorious *songket* (brocade textiles) once woven by the Minangkabau. Both the buffalo and the duck are important in their iconography: the buffalo is depicted as a pair of horns and represents bravery, and the duck symbolizes co-operation and the homecoming wanderer, and is represented by an 'S' shape. Motifs of bamboo shoots and areca-nut palms are also carved, in deference to the natural world.

The Minangkabau houses are made of wood, with the exception of the rear longitudinal wall, which is simply a plain lattice woven in a chequered pattern out of split bamboo. The roof is of a truss and cross-beam structure, and is thatched with *ijuk.* The thatch is laid in bundles that can easily be made to fit the curves of the roof peaks. Roof finials are drawn into points said to resemble buffalo horns – an allusion to a legend concerning a bullfight from which the Minangkabau name is thought to have derived. The roof peaks themselves are built up out of many small battens and rafters.

The *rumah gadang,* the traditional great communal house, is a broad structure set on wooden pillars. The main doorway leading into the centre of the house is surmounted by a perpendicular porchway with a triangular gable and a dramatically upsweeping peaked ridge end. Its plan is rectangular, with a projection at each end usually made up of three tiers, each of which has different floor levels. The roofing consists of five elements each inserted into each other. The sleeping quarters of the women who share the house are alcoves (by custom uneven in number) set in a row against the rear wall, and are curtained off from the great interior space that forms the main living area. The whole house is raised on wooden pillars that can be as tall as 3 metres (10 ft), and a verandah runs along the front face of the house, used as a reception and dining area, and as a sleeping place for guests and the youngest and oldest members of the family. Typically, the original *rumah gadang* will be surrounded by newer ones built for married sisters and daughters of the parent family. The women's maternal uncle is responsible for making sure that each marriageable woman in the family has a room of her own. He does this either by building a new house or more commonly by adding annexes to the original one. It is said that the number of married daughters in a home can be told by counting the horn-like extensions to it. These are not always added symmetrically, sometimes making the *rumah gadang* look rather unbalanced.

The more opulent houses have high walls and multiple roofs supported by great interior wooden piers. Cooking and storage areas are often in separate buildings, and adolescent boys will live in yet another building known as a *mussalah*. The Minangkabau royal palace at Pagarruyung has three roofs which rise in tiers, the first two laterally and the top room transversely. Extensions at either side add a further two roof forms, increasing the dramatic impact of the structure.

Nias is a large, rugged island lying off the west coast of Sumatra, opposite Sibolga. The Niassans were a megalithic, head-hunting society whose economy was based on agriculture and pig-rearing, supplemented by the export of slaves captured in intervillage warfare. Within a rigidly stratified society, the chiefs, particularly in the south of the island, had access to a wealth of material resources and human labour. With the riches thus generated, at the beginning of the twentieth century the chiefs in the villages of southern Nias built themselves *omo sebua*, houses on massive ironwood pillars, with towering roofs. The ironwood pillars rest on stone slabs and are braced both laterally and longitudinally, with diagonal beams of the same dimensions and material. This enhances flexibility and stability in this earthquake-prone region. The houses are virtually impregnable to attack, as they can be entered only through a tiny trap door reached by a

A wooden panel on a house in Bawomataluo village in south Nias.

An ancestor figure, helmet crest and male and female earrings carved on an ebony house panel in Bawomataluo.

narrow staircase in the middle of the piers. They were built to intimidate, and the steeply pitched roofs alone soar up to a height of 16 metres (50 ft); the gables project dramatically at both the front and rear, providing both shade and shelter from the driving tropical rain and giving the building a hooded, awesome appearance.

Southern Nias villages are built on strategic hilltops reached by steep stone stairways and laid out either in one long street or to a cruciform plan. Villages are large, holding up to five thousand people (in the slave-raiding past, smaller villages would not have been defensible). The *omo sebua* is situated in the centre of the village, and in front of it are exquisitely carved, monolithic sacrificial stone slabs. At Bawomataluo the *bale*, the public meeting hall which is the second most important and second largest building, lies slightly to one side of the central crossroads. Opposite the *bale*, to the left of the *omo sebua*, is the 2.7 metre (9 ft) 'jumping stone', where the village youth used to train for slave-taking raids, jumping over its spiked top as if it were the stockade of another village. Commoners' houses are built to a rectangular plan, as is the *omo sebua*, and are crammed close together in terraces on either side of the streets. Interior connect-

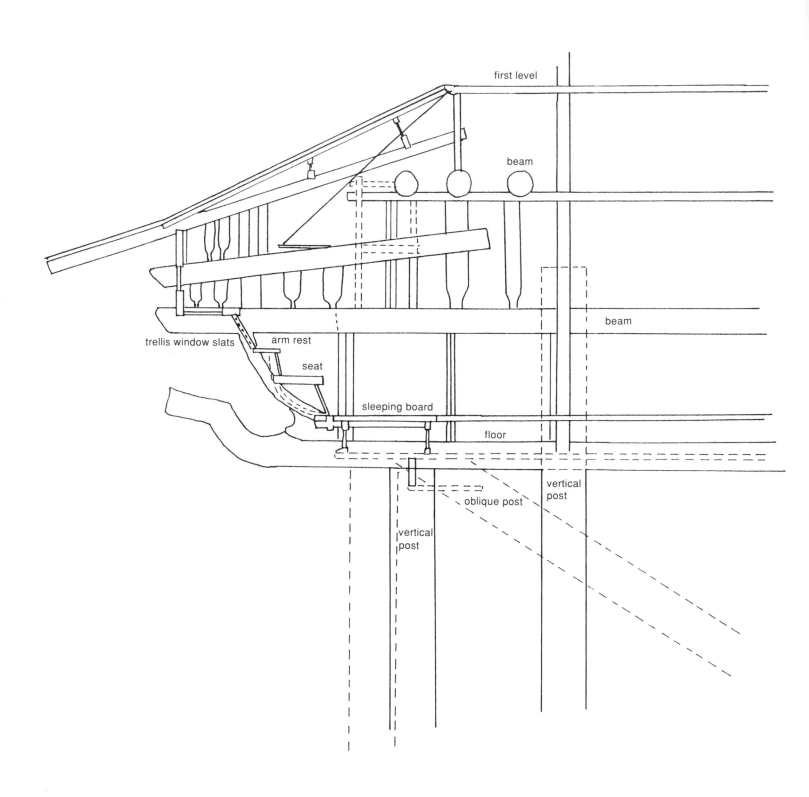

Opposite *Section of the* omo sebua, *the chief's house, in Bawomataluo village, south Nias.*

ing doors enable villagers to walk the whole length of the terrace without setting foot on the paved street below, most useful if the village came under attack. The houses, including those of the aristocracy, are equipped with bowed galleries set underneath the projecting front gable (their design is presumed to have been derived from the bulbous sterns of Dutch galleons). The galleries provided a vantage point from which to repel attackers and, in times of peace, a convenient, cool and comfortable place for observing the street life below.

Interiors are of planed hardwood (often ebony) boards, highly polished and set into each other with tongue-and-grooving, often incorporating bas-relief carvings of ancestors, jewelry, animals, fish and boats. Each tableau contains a balance of female and male elements so essential to Indonesian cosmic harmony. The great houses are decorated with freestanding wooden carvings – of monkeys eating fruit, for example – and the rafters are festooned with the jaw bones of the pigs that were sacrificed for the workers' feast when the house was completed. The *omo sebua* at Bawomataluo has a carved ebony throne set into the wall of its large front room, which once contained an ancestor figure (removed after the coming of Christianity). It also has hundreds of these pigs' jaw bones hung up on its rafters, which serve as an indication of the size of the labour force needed to build such an edifice.

The chief's house is a structure of complex symbolism (see p.14). The nine levels inside the roof are said to correspond to the nine levels of heaven. Human sacrifice was deemed necessary to obtain the requisite cosmic balance before the house could be formally completed and occupied: the corner pillars could only be erected after a head dedicated to the god of the netherworld was placed under them. More heads were offered to the god of the upperworld when the top roof beam was put in place. Macabre carvings on the sacrificial stone megaliths outside the *omo sebua* indicate that slaves were buried alive underneath them. All these ceremonies involving human sacrifice and head-hunting are now things of the past – outlawed by the Dutch, they are now morally alien to the strictly Christian Niassan villagers. With the demise of their war-like, bloodthirsty society, the need for symbolic or defensible structures has disappeared. Increasingly, Niassans are living outside their strategically located villages, in modern houses; but despite all this, they are still immensely proud of their unique cultural heritage and of their architecture.

The ancestors of the south Nias people were immigrants from central Nias. House styles there resemble those of south Nias but are simpler, and lack the characteristic south Nias projecting curved front. Traditional houses in north Nias are built to an oval plan and resemble southern houses in their use of diagonal piles and the ventilation flap cut into the roof.

The Sumatrans, with their rich cultural diversity, are architects of some of the most outstanding examples of Indonesian vernacular building. In the saddle-backed houses of the Minangkabau and the Toba Batak, Sumatra possesses some of the prime examples of Dong-Son-derived housing in the whole of South-East Asia. The *rumah adat* of the Karo Batak and the *omo sebua* of Nias represent some of the world's most impressive wooden buildings. The grace and airy comfort of the houses of Aceh, the east coast and the south are the pride of Malay culture in Sumatra. Although the young are increasingly turning to modern Indonesian architectural forms, and television and video culture fast encroaches, the different tribal and ethnic groups still place great value on the *rumah adat*.

The traditional ancestral home is the most visible symbol of Indonesian cultural identity, the link with a past that predates the major world religions, and joins the immigrant of the *merantau* to his village of origin. Sumatran traditional housing will continue as long as these distinctive and vital cultures endure. The vernacular architecture of this vast and varied island is a tribute to the skill of the carpenters and villagers who have built these houses and to the vision of the chiefs and rich immigrants who continue to commission them.

3
Java, Bali and Lombok
The Teeming Heartland

JAVA AND BALI together form the heartland of Indonesia. They are by far the most densely populated islands in the archipelago, and are also its cultural and, in the case of Java, its political focus. Although these islands profess different religious beliefs – Java is Muslim whilst Bali practises its own, very idiosyncratic version of Hindu-Buddhism – an all-pervasive belief in spirits and semi-deified ancestors persists in both places. They share common traditions in dance, music and theatre, and folk iconography derived from the Hindu epics of the *Mahabharata* and the *Ramayana* features in both cultures. Strong similarities are also evident in their vernacular architecture. Unusually within Indonesia, Javanese and Balinese houses are ground-built, and made of brick, tiles and other types of masonry as well as wood. Lombok, the small island that neighbours Bali to the east, has large Balinese settlements in its western half which share the same building tradition, and has other cultural affinities with Bali. The indigenous Sasaks also erect ground-built houses.

Java is a densely populated island of tiny rice-fields and towering volcanoes, sprawling polluted modern cities and rather staid centres of traditional culture. It is by far the most important component in the Indonesian enigma. A long, narrow island stretching from the straits of Sunda in the west to the straits of Bali in the east, Java is divided culturally and linguistically into three areas. The people who live in the central and eastern parts of the island are Javanese, whereas the western population is Sundanese. Madura, another long, thin, but smaller island, lies close to Java's north-east coast. Madura is predominantly Islamic in outlook, as is western Java, but the inhabitants of east and central Java, although Muslim as well, are deeply mystical, and hold a firm belief in all manner of spirits and demons.

With its rich volcanic soil, Java supports around 65% (about 110 million) of Indonesia's population. As well as being the central power in Indonesia, it is the focus of most of its economic and educational activity – through the long centuries of colonization, the Dutch concentrated most intensively on Java, and the great majority of Indonesia's industries and educational institutions are consequently located here. Most of the wealth of the archipelago is ineluctably drawn to Java, and to Jakarta especially, and the island is very receptive to the influences of the industrialized world. The deep historical roots of Javanese culture, however, are unrivalled anywhere else in Indonesia. A Hindu kingdom was first established on the island by the fifth century AD, although Indian traders had first reached Java some three hundred years before. Hindu and Buddhist ideas and practices spread fast amongst the Javanese ruling classes, who were in part attracted by certain socio-religious concepts pertaining to these faiths.

The architectural legacy of Hindu-Buddism is to be found all over the island. The remains of stone and brick *candi* (temples) are a constant reminder of its Hindu past, and the great stepped pyramid-shaped Buddhist monument of Borobudur, built some time between AD 750 and 850, is striking testimony to a highly sophisticated culture. Throughout tropical South-East Asia, the only surviving archaeological remains are stone or brick public buildings such as these, but it is evident from the sites of ancient cities such as Angkor Thom in Cambodia that wooden structures of one form or another must have occupied the large areas between the great monuments.

Remnants of a Javanese vernacular tradition that conforms to the general Indonesian style of pile-built dwellings can be found in the Badui culture in the far west of Java. The Badui are thought to be descended from the Sundanese Hindu aristocracy of the Pajajaran kingdom, who fled from invading Muslim forces in the fifteenth century. Their houses in the isolated hill districts above Banten and a few others near Garut are the only remaining examples of Dong-Son-influenced traditional domestic architecture in Java.

The current form of domestic architecture was established in the Majapahit era of the fourteenth century. It consists of a single room with posts supporting the roof, and a surrounding yard. The floor is of mud and the walls of woven split bamboo. The more prosperous farmsteads have structures for sheltering livestock and storing feed, enclosed by a brick wall or a bamboo fence. The structure of most village houses is highly standardized, comprising a basic rectangular unit wider than it is deep, set on an earth foundation about 30 centimetres (one foot) high, revetted with brick. It has a ridged roof running the width of the house. The front eaves are usually extended to form a shallow porch, and the door is set centrally in the front of the house; a smaller one at the side or rear gives access to the kitchen. Floors are usually made of packed earth, roofs of ceramic tiles, walls of woven split bamboo as sturdy as can be afforded. The components and size of the house vary according to the wealth of the owner. The uprights of the timber frame that supports the roof are, if possible, teak but more commonly cheaper coconut wood. The poorer houses have loose-packed earth floors, and flimsy bamboo walls. Richer families live in houses composed of two basic units set back to back with thick bamboo or brick walls and a more complex roof structure. The interior is usually divided up by interwoven split bamboo partitions. All houses have one largish room for receiving guests and for living and working.

At the back of the house are sleeping areas, each with a sleeping platform or bed. Husband, wife and baby sleep in one, children in the others. The kitchen is usually a small outhouse tacked on to the side or rear of the main unit. If the

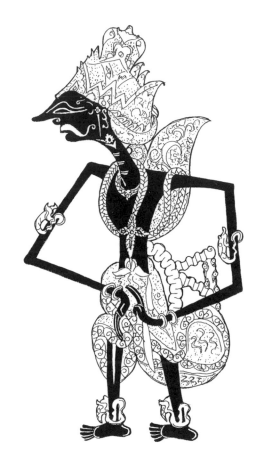

Wayang figure of Krishna painted on a house panel in Surakarta, central Java.

Borobudur, central Java.

owners are rich enough to afford a second unit at the rear, this will house the sleeping chambers as well as an inner living room where more intimate guests can be received. In richer houses, the middle room of the rear unit is built with brick walls and a concrete floor and will have an ornate carved wooden door. Here the family valuables are kept safe from thieves. Houses are sparsely furnished, with sometimes only a square wooden table and four chairs.

The techniques for building traditional houses are familiar to every adult male in the village. When a new house is being constructed, all the community will help out in return for food while the work is in progress, and in expectation of help in return when it is needed. The standard design and simple construction make it easy to extend the house (or even to sell bits off when times are hard). The basic unit of the smaller house can be deepened with additional uprights to extend the walls and the roof at the front and back, and an external kitchen can be built on.

Distinctions of wealth and social status are indicated by variations of this basic plan. The houses of the more affluent are composed of at least four areas. These are the *pendopo*, a large open pavilion for the reception of guests, a small intermediate area known as the *pringgitan*, reserved for the owner of the house, and the *dalem*, the rear of the house, which contains the *sentong*, a ceremonial area which forms the spiritual core of every Javanese home. Other rooms are, of course, often added to this central core, as well as a kitchen, bathrooms and outhouses used as stables and for craftwork.

The house and outbuildings are surrounded by a wall, and another wall is built in line with the front wall of the *dalem* to divide off the public areas from those at the rear, which are strictly private. The area surrounding a Javanese house is normally planted with coconut palms and tall fruit trees, which not only supply fruits but also firewood. These trees serve the vital function of providing the villagers with shade from the sun and protection from the heavy rain.

Regional variations occur not so much in the basic plan but more in the roof structure. In Sunda, west Java, the roof is made up of two or three two-sided parallel elements with gables aligned on the narrower sides. In central Java the roof is made up of three sections. The central part is composed of two planes, then on each side of that is a roof with a shallower slope. Houses in east Java and Madura are based on the central Javanese model. The most common variant has a hipped roof with the planes of the central part steeply pitched, a shallower sloped roof edging it and continuing all round the house. Traditional housing in Java differs little within each region, apart from the variations required to distinguish the wealth and status of the builder.

Java has less traditional housing than anywhere else in Indonesia. The majority of the Javanese now live in bungalows with brick or concrete walls set on concrete foundations, and tiled or zinc roofs. The aspiration of the many poor, rural Javanese is to imitate the lifestyle of the Jakarta elite that they see on the television every day. The socially conservative, cohesive forces that maintain the traditional house are less strong in Java, which has undergone centuries of uninterrupted change through foreign influence. In Java, the traditional house is regarded as an object of interest, to be looked upon and perhaps admired, but not to be imitated. The future lies elsewhere.

Bali, once a fabled tropical paradise, is now a vastly popular tourist destination. It had, until twenty years ago, one of the most complex, many-layered social structures in Indonesia. This was a product of the riches and population growth generated by the island's abundantly fertile rice fields; it also resulted from the superimposition of another layer of ruling aristocracy onto the native one by the Hindu Javanese courts which fled to Bali to escape Muslim domination at the fall of the Majapahit Empire in the fifteenth century. The vernacular

A stone panel depicting a pile-built house with an angled gable, Borobudur, central Java.

architectural tradition in Bali is a reflection of this cultural and religious complexity.

Of all the Indonesian islanders, the Balinese have the most highly refined sense of place and orientation, in terms of both cardinal points and geographical features such as the sea and the mountains, which are of great importance. The requirements of correct spatial orientation determine the layout of house and village and dominate daily life: there are auspicious places to eat, cook, sleep and even have sexual intercourse, and a Balinese person must lie in a certain direction to sleep. The axis of Balinese orientation is drawn between the mountains and the sea. *Kaja* means upstream, or towards the mountain, *kelod* downstream, or towards the sea. *Kangin* (east) and *kauh* (west) and the other compass points are also of vital importance. The exact direction of *kaja* and *kelod*, of course, varies according to a village's location. *Kaja* is to the south in north Bali, but to the north in south Bali. The direction of the mountains is holy and prestigious, but in the seaward direction is considered to lie the home of threatening demons – despite the fact that Bali is surrounded by sea and fish are an important part of the Balinese diet.

Most Balinese live in villages (even though they may now work in large towns or cities such as Denpasar), and the layout of the village is of vital importance. First of all, the orientation of the three temples around which the component parts of the village are grouped must be determined. The important 'temple of origin', the *pura puseh* which is dedicated to Vishnu, the god of the mountain streams, will be sited in the direction of the mountains. The temple of the great meeting hall, the *pura bale agung*, is located in the centre of the village, and to the 'unclean' seaward side of the village is placed the *pura dalem*, the temple of the unpurified dead and associated, potentially dangerous, spirits. The *pura dalem* is dedicated to Siva the destroyer. Yet further to the seaside is the cemetery. The residential part of the village, the *banjar*, occupies the area between the *pura puseh* and the *pura desa,* the village temple dedicated to Brahma. The *banjar* is divided up into different neighbourhoods that are named according to their location (east, west or centre) or the caste that lives there. Bali retains the Hindu caste divisions of *brahmana* (priest), *satria* (royalty), *wesia* (warrior), and *sudra* (artisan or peasant); the *banjar brahmana*, for example, is where the priests live, and the *banjar pande* where the smiths live. Each *banjar* has its own *bale banjar*, a meeting hall with a drum tower for summoning its members. Every villager is a member of a particular *banjar* and the male heads of families meet at the *bale banjar* to plan, for example, the co-operative harvesting of rice, the communal working of the extremely complex irrigation system, the repair of temples and the organization of village feasts. The *banjar* has a cultural and religious role and provides banking services for its members. It also has a political function, its leaders being able to express their views to the village chief, the *kepala desa,* who can then pass on the information to the higher echelons of the civil government. In contrast to the open arrangement of the village, Balinese homes invariably consist of a number of small structures grouped together and surrounded by a walled courtyard to ensure privacy. The way in which these small buildings are distributed around the courtyard is an indication not only of the wealth and status of the owner but also of his caste. A nobleman's house will differ in layout from that of the *brahmanas*, which will in turn be different from that of the *sudras*, who make up the overwhelming majority of the Balinese population.

The *pekarangan* (compound) of the *kuren*, the Balinese home, is made up of five basic elements: the doorway, with its screen and split arch, the main sleeping area, with its open verandah, a raised barn for storing rice, a kitchen and a bathing area. There may also be a workshop and a family temple. Theoretically, but rarely in practice, the courtyard is divided up into nine equal parts. If *kaja*, the mountainside direction, is taken as north, the family temple is always placed in the north-east corner of the courtyard. The adjacent south-east corner is considered to be the abode of evil and is always left empty. The entrance should face the auspicious south-west, but often this is not possible. The *lumbung* (granary) and the *paon* (kitchen) are placed in the south-west corner, to the right of some-

A cili *figure, which depicts Dewi Sri, the Balinese rice goddess, made of woven palm leaf.*

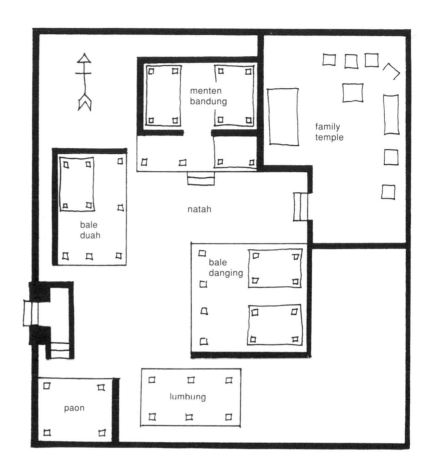

Plan of a house compound, south Bali, showing the orientation of the living, ritual and storage areas.

one entering the courtyard. To the incomer's left, situated around the *natah*, the centre of the courtyard which is left open to provide a work and recreational area for the family, are three distinct sleeping quarters. Clockwise from an incomer's left are the *bale duah* (guests' room) parallel to the west wall, the *menten bandung* (the room for parents, grandparents and unmarried girls) parallel to the north wall, and the *bale danging* (the adults' quarters) parallel to the east wall. An additional *bale*, the *bale delod*, may be constructed on the *kelod* ('south') side if required. The *bale danging* is used to celebrate such important rites of passage as weddings and tooth-filing. Children sleep in the *bale duah* or in a special pavilion built for them in the north-west corner of the compound.

The word *bale* means 'pavilion', and the structure of the *bale* is at least partially open (the even, humid climate means that a roof to provide shelter from the rain is the only real necessity). They will have one or two walls, but the pavilion where the head of the compound resides (with all the family treasures) will be enclosed on all four sides. The pavilions are distinguished from one another by the number of pillars (*sasaka*) each has. A six-pillar *bale* is known as a *bale sakenam* and the largest *bale*, with twelve pillars, is known as a *bale gede*. The *bale danging* is usually a *bale gede*. These buildings are constructed with posts set into a masonry base supporting a roof of radiating beamwork. Some have walls of brick or tuff masonry, a feature that probably derived from the temple architecture of medieval east Java. The roof is always crowned with a terracotta finial.

Some roofs are still made of *alang-alang* grass, sewn onto the ribs of coconut-palm leaves, which are set closely together and tied onto the bamboo or coconut-wood roof frame with hard-wearing sugar-palm fibre. Layers of grass thatch are combed with a special rake, then trimmed, and extra layers of grass are added at the four corners. This type of thatch, often 45 centimetres (18 in.) thick, can last for up to fifty years. Nowadays a ceramic tiled roof is more usual (although bamboo is an alternative in the mountains). The beams that support the roof are fitted together and held in place with pegs made from the heartwood of coconut trees. Wooden or stone carvings of protective spirits can commonly be seen over doorways.

Rice barns are the only Balinese buildings that are raised on piles. These piles are topped with large wooden discs just below the main body of the granary to prevent rats from getting in. The barns are thatched with rice straw or *alang-alang* grass.

All traditional-style Balinese construction follows the prescribed methods laid down in various treatises on building, some of which date back to the fifteenth century. Anyone wishing to build will first commission a master builder, an *udangi*. After discussing the specifics of the commission, the *udangi* will first take the client's measurements, and then transfer them onto his bamboo measuring stick. From these are derived the units of measure that determine the dimensions of the compound and the *sasaka*. Firstly there is the *depa*, which is the distance between the middle fingers when each arm is fully extended to the side. The distance from the tip of the outstretched middle finger to the elbow, known as the *hasta* (equivalent to the Western cubit) is also added to the measuring stick. The *depa* and the *hasta* together are equal to the basic wall measurement unit, which is also added to the stick. According to the old treatises, however, a small adjustment must be made to increase each unit of measurement slightly. This is known as the *urip*, and is thought necessary to bring the building alive upon completion. In the case of the *depa*, the *urip* is the width of the fist with the thumb extended. The three units of measurement added together make the *depa asti musti*, which is the unit for laying out the compound walls. The corners of the compound are then staked out to the dimensions appropriate both to the client's caste and to the location. The next important job is the cutting and then the setting up of the *sasaka*.

Opposite 59 The tiled roofs of the royal city of Jogjakarta in central Java. Jogjakarta is a great centre for the arts, and a focus for Javanese batik production, music and dance.

The long and narrow island of Java is home to more than half of Indonesia's population, and it is also the cultural and political centre of the archipelago. Its sprawling cities are for the most part modern and polluted, but some remain centres of traditional culture. The basic architectural unit throughout Java is a single room with posts supporting the roof. The floors are of mud, roofs of ceramic tiles and the walls of brick or woven split bamboo. This basic unit can be added to with ease. **60** The roof forms and ceramic tiles of the houses that line this alleyway in Jogjakarta are typical of central Javanese domestic architecture. **61** A bale, or pavilion, whose tiled roof is supported by concentric rings of wooden pillars. **62** A house in the backstreets of Jogjakarta, with a bird-cage hung from the eaves. **63** The teak beam structure supporting the roof of a bale in Jogjakarta.

60 △

61 △

62 △

63 ▷

Indian traders first came to Java in the second century AD, and a Hindu kingdom had been established there by the fifth century. The courts of Java were sympathetic to many Buddhist as well as Hindu concepts and practices, and the religions spread rapidly. The architectural legacy of Hindu-Buddhism is to be found all over the island. The remains of stone and brick temples are a constant reminder of the Hindu past, and the great stepped pyramid-shaped Buddhist monument of Borobudur is striking testimony to a highly sophisticated culture. The inheritors of this distinguished architectural tradition founded the central Javanese sultanates of Jogjakarta and Surakarta. **64** Carved stone hero figures from Trowulan in east Java, the last capital of the Majapahit Empire. **65, 66** The interior and front facade of Taman Sari, the old water-palace in Jogjakarta, which was built between 1758 and 1765. It has long fallen into disuse. **67** A naga – a mythical dragon-like creature, to which great powers are attributed – decorating the balustrade of the water-palace. **68** Carved and painted wooden barriers surmounted by a demonic face and snakes, in the reception hall of the royal kraton (palace) at Jogjakarta.

64 △

65 △

66 △   67 ▽   68 ▽

69 △   70 △   71 ▽

72 △

The legendary tropical paradise of Bali is now a thriving centre of tourism. Until recently, the structure of Balinese society was one of the most complex in Indonesia, a consequence of the population growth and wealth generated by the island's abundantly fertile rice fields. This was compounded by the arrival of the Hindu aristocracy from Java, fleeing Islam at the fall of the Majapahit Empire. The vernacular architectural tradition in Bali is a reflection of this cultural and religious complexity. **69** A temple bell-tower and a lean-to motor-cycle shed made with thatch and bamboo in Denpasar, Bali's capital city. **70** A house in Ubud, the cultural centre of Bali, with brick and carved stone walls and decaying rice-straw thatch in need of refurbishment. **71** A carved wooden doorway in Ubud, with richly ornamental floral carving. **72** Temple musicians sitting beneath a bell-tower with a two-tiered thatched roof, in Denpasar. **73** A carved and painted Garuda, the winged mount of the Hindu god Vishnu, and wooden vaulting, in a restaurant in Kuta on Bali's southern coast.

73 △

The siting of buildings is of primary importance all over Indonesia, but especially in Bali. Not only the points of the compass but also geographical features will bear upon the location and alignment of a building. The proximity of the sea and the mountains determines the orientation of the three temples that form the nucleus of the village. The residential part of the village, the banjar, is grouped around these temples. **74, 75** Beyond a carved tuff gateway in Ubud is a temple with a tiered thatched roof and brick and carved tuff walls. **76** A brick and carved tuff gateway to a carved and gilded temple door is crowned with a demonic figure and flanked by stone guardian spirits. **77** A bas-relief carved tuff panel depicting monkeys and human figures, in the brick wall of a temple. **78** Carved tuff figures of guardian spirits and naga dragons adorned with offerings of buleng (chequered cloth) and flowers.

75 △

◁74

76 △

77 △

78 △

79 △

80 △

81 △

The Sasak villages of Lombok are clustered
on low escarpments to conserve scarce
arable land. Traditional houses are
ground-built with wooden frames and
thatched with alang-alang grass. They are
grouped around a mosque situated at the
centre of the village. **79** These rice barns,
which are made with alang-alang thatch
and interwoven split bamboo wall
panelling, belong to a house in Sade village,
southern Lombok. **80** A woman weaving
on a backstrap loom beneath a lumbung
(rice-barn). **81** Alang-alang thatching on
the roof ridge of a house in Sade village.
The layer of thatch between the ridge beam
and purlins seals off the roof ridge. **82**
Bundles of alang-alang grass are tied to
battens for the thatching of a lumbung.
Overleaf **83** A traditional Sasak house
with an alang-alang thatched roof, a
wooden trellis and an interwoven split
bamboo porch. A lumbung stands disused
in the background.

84 △

The pride of Sasak vernacular architecture is the lumbung, *the pile-built, bonnet-roofed rice barn. These rice barns are set in rows along the more easily accessible lower pathways. The village then rises above them in tiers to the crown of the hill, with many zig-zag trails leading up between the houses.* **84** A lumbung *with a typically Sasak bonnet-shaped roof. The storage area of the granary has a flap in it into which the dried padi is shovelled twice a year after harvest. A lean-to shed has been added to it to extend the space available for weaving.* **85** *A waterpot and storage hut, both raised on wooden pillars.* **86** *A Sade villager is building a new house. He has already made the packed earth plinth for the central part, and erected the house and roof frame. He is now preparing the mud and buffalo-dung floor for the lower porch.*

85 △

86 ▷

Opposite 87 *Weaving* lurik, *a striped cloth, in the shaded undercroft of a* lumbung, *Sade village, southern Lombok.*

Sasaka are usually tenoned at the base and fitted into a socketed, cast foundation or precast foundation block. If the *sasaka* are going to support platforms, holes to receive the loadbearing beams are mortised into them. These wooden platforms with bamboo slats are used as eating areas for guests during the day and for sleeping on at night. *Sasaka* are usually about 10 centimetres (4 in.) square but can vary in height from 1.8 metres (6 ft) to 2.5 metres (8 ft). They are square in section from the base up to the midway point, which is marked with a carved design known as a *paduraksa*. From this point upwards, the corners are bevelled off so that they become octagonal in cross section. The junction of the *sasaka* and the rafters is also marked with a carving. Teak, which is either grown in the vicinity or more usually imported from Kalimantan or Java, is preferred for *sasaka*. The pillars of a shrine or temple, however, must be cut from a tree growing locally, to which the prescribed offerings have first been made. The base of the *sasaka* is always the root end – the heaviest end – of the tree. To determine which end this is, the wood is balanced at its midpoint on a piece of ready-cut timber, or floated in water.

Before construction begins, certain ceremonies must be performed. For sacred buildings, the *panca datu*, five metals (gold, silver, bronze, iron and copper), are buried in the foundations, along with a coconut wrapped around with five differently coloured threads. For secular buildings, the ceremony simply consists of burying bricks wrapped in white cloth. The day of the ceremony and the day on which construction starts must be astrologically auspicious. There are other ceremonies that are conducted at various stages of the building, but the most important is the *melaspas*, the purificatory rite of completion, which brings the previously 'dead' materials alive as a living house. The house now has feet, body and a head – the foundations, the pillars and the roof.

Of all the Indonesian islands, with perhaps the exception of Java, Bali has been most changed by outside influence, yet, paradoxically, it retains more of its old customs than anywhere else in the archipelago. No doubt this is in part to counteract the ever-increasing numbers of foreign tourists that flood into Denpasar airport every day; but it should not be forgotten that the Balinese have a shrewd business sense, and their attachment to cultural traditions may also be in recognition of the fact that this is what attracts the tourist.

Consequently, although the layout of a Balinese village may not have changed, the houses themselves may be built in a variety of styles, and modern materials will in some cases have replaced traditional ones. Foundations are often now of concrete, and the floors tiled. Walls may be of concrete blocks rather than brick or limestone, and concrete pillars are used instead of teak. In the hotels and restaurants of Kuta and Sanur, however, among the most popular tourist resorts of the island, traditional Balinese building styles, materials and techniques are much in evidence.

A karang Ceviri, *a protective demon, carved in stone and set above an important gateway, in Bali.*

The Balinese people's reverence for their culture and their religion runs extremely deep. They will ignore the requirements of business if a religious or social festivity is to be observed. Balinese traditional architecture is changing, but its future seems unclear on an island so flooded with tourists. All the old techniques of building are still keenly practised in the rural areas as well as in the tourist centres. Perhaps the future of vernacular architecture in Bali lies in a blend of the modern and the traditional; the only certainty is that the architectural future will be imbued with the natural Balinese sense of taste, style and fine craftsmanship. It will certainly be prosperous.

A Chinese-influenced pattern incised on a screen in Karangasem, Bali.

Lombok lies immediately to the east of Bali. It is approximately the same size, but differs markedly in climate and terrain. The main area of habitation is the central plain between the mountainous north of the island and the barren, arid south. There is a substantial contingent of Balinese living in west Lombok. The majority of indigenous Muslim and animist Sasaks inhabit the drier, eastern part of the island. The houses and temples of the Lombok Balinese are similar in design to those of their homeland, but of great interest are the Sasak traditional houses that rise in tiers up the hot, bare hills of Lombok's southern peninsula. Though largely fallen into desuetude in the more accessible and more developed parts of the island, in southern Lombok they are still lived in. This is not only because the villagers are proud of their culture (and cannot anyway afford to change their way of life), but also for the reason that it is in their financial interest to maintain, repair and reconstruct in the traditional style as the island becomes increasingly attractive to tourists.

Villages are clustered on low escarpments not so much for defensive purposes but more to conserve scarce arable land. Access to a village is via a pathway leading to a narrow roofed gateway. The village then rises to the crown of the hill and usually continues over the other side, with a few lateral pathways and many zigzag trails leading up between the houses.

The central feature of the village is a bamboo and thatch mosque, built in the Malay style with a square pyramid or double pyramid roof, but the pride of Sasak vernacular architecture is the *lumbung*, a pile-built, bonnet-roofed rice barn. The *lumbung* rice barns are set in rows along the more easily accessible lower pathways. The only opening to the *lumbung* is a high window, into which the rice is ladled. The barn is filled twice a year (the traditional long-stemmed rice has a five-month growing period). Two, three or four *lumbung*, each owned by a separate family, are set end to end with a few metres between them. Four 1.5 metre (5 ft) hardwood posts are mounted on a level, sundried mud and buffalo-dung platform. Discs known as *jelepreng* are set near the top of these posts to prevent rodents from getting in to the rice store. The posts carry two lateral beams, on which rests a cantilevered frame supporting the bamboo rafters. The shape of the granary is determined by this bonnet-like frame given to each barn face. The thatch consists of locally gathered *alang-alang* grass, its bound ends intertwined with flexible laths of green bamboo and woven into stiff bulky battens. As with the rest of Indonesia, the undercroft of the granaries acts as a social gathering place, particularly for women and children, and provides a shaded area for weaving. For good luck, and to ensure the protection of the forces of the indigenous Wektu Telu religion, old Chinese coins are imbedded in a disc of matted *ijuk* fibre and placed beneath each post. Houses in Sasak villages are built co-operatively. Specialist carpenters may receive payment, but other members of the village offer their labour freely, although they are fed while work is in progress.

Traditional houses are divided into two distinct areas with separate functions, set at different levels but covered with a common roof. The higher area is built on a raised rectangular plinth of packed mud and dung compound, which rises approximately 1.2 metres (4 ft) above the other, larger mud and dung platform, which will act as a porch. Hardwood posts 1.5 metres (5 ft) high are erected at each corner of the rectangular plinth. These support the ring beam that carries the hipped roof, with its post-and-beam structure of local hardwood, and rafters and purlins of bamboo culms. The spaces between the original four corner posts that support the ring beam are walled off with interlaced split bamboo and a sliding lockable door of hardwood known as *Temus*, which once grew in the vicinity. This forms a secure storage and sleeping area. Once the kitchen was incorporated into this interior space, making it yet darker and dingier, and of course full of smoke.

On three sides, the eaves of the house descend almost to the ground, being walled off with interwoven split bamboo or mud, or a combination of the two. These low walls now enclose a low kitchen and to some extent contain the smoke. The bamboo rafters on the downhill face of the roof are extended to enclose the lower terrace, which is used as a social area during the day and a place for men to sleep at night. This lower porch is usually reached by two or three earthen steps and fenced off from the adjoining pathway by a wall or more usually an open bamboo lattice.

By the side of the Sasak *rumah adat* is a house made of traditional materials but with a hipped roof supported by a wooden frame, with interwoven split bamboo walls standing about 1.8 metres (6 ft) high on a single, low, mud and dung plinth. This style of house is often now preferred, as it offers more comfortable living accommodation, but the living and sleeping areas are not so clearly defined, and there is less overall space. Nails are now used as reinforcements, and rafters and thatch are tied with *ijuk* fibre or dried bamboo leaf.

4
Borneo and Sulawesi
Home of Tribes and Ancestors

BORNEO AND SULAWESI are two great islands found to the north of Java and Bali. Both have an abundance of natural resources, and their traditional architecture, along with the rest of their indigenous culture, is rich and varied. Sulawesi lies between Borneo and the Moluccas. It has a strangely contorted shape, seemingly composed only of peninsulas, and when the pioneering Portuguese first encountered it in the early sixteenth century, they thought it was a group of islands and named it the Celebese. Sulawesi is home to some of the most distinctive and important ethnic groups in the archipelago. The sea-faring, once piratical Islamic Bugis and Makassarese of the south-west, along with the strongly Christian Minahasa of the northern peninsula, are the dominant forces within the island, but it is the culture of the Christian and animist Toraja of the rugged mountainous central highlands that gives Sulawesi its unique colour.

Toraja is a name of Bugis origin given to the different peoples of the mountainous regions of the northern part of the south peninsula, which have remained isolated until quite recently. Their native religion is megalithic and animistic, and is characterized by animal sacrifices, ostentatious funeral rites and huge communal feasts. The Toraja only began to lose faith in their religion after 1909, when Protestant missionaries arrived in the wake of the Dutch colonizers. Nowadays roughly 60% of the Toraja are Christian, and 10% are Muslim; the rest hold in some measure to their original religion. Whatever their religious belief, it is their ancestral home, their 'house of origin', the great *banua Toraja* with its saddleback roof and dramatically upswept roof ridge ends, that is the cultural focus for every Toraja. This house of origin is also known as a *tongkonan*, a name derived from the Toraja word for 'to sit'; it literally means the place where family members meet – to discuss important affairs, to take part in ceremonies and to make arrangements for the refurbishment of the house.

The Toraja are divided up geographically into different groups, the most important of which are the Mamasa, who are centred around the isolated Kalumpang valley, and the Sa'dan of the southern Toraja lands. There have never been any strong, lasting political groupings within the Toraja. The Sa'dan area, with its market towns of Makale and Rantepao, is known as Tana Toraja. Good roads now reach Tana Toraja from Ujung Panjang, the capital of Sulawesi, bringing a large seasonal influx of foreign tourists who, whilst injecting money into the local economy, have not yet had much lasting affect on local people's lives.

In former times, Toraja villages were sited strategically on hilltops and fortified to such an extent that sometimes access was only possible through tunnels bored through rock. This was all part of the then common Indonesian custom of head-hunting and inter-village raids. The Dutch pacified the Toraja and forced them to leave the hills and to build their villages in the valleys, and they also introduced wet-rice cultivation. The Toraja abandoned their traditional slash-and-burn agricultural policy and now live by rice-farming, and raising pigs and beautiful buffalo.

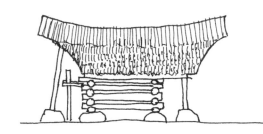

The Toraja are a proto-Malay people whose origins lie in mainland South-East Asia (possibly Cambodia). Toraja legends claim that they arrived from the north by sea. Caught in a violent storm, their boats were so damaged as to be unseaworthy, so instead they used them as roofs for their new homes. The *tongkonan*, with their boat-shaped roofs, always face towards the north.

Tongkonan are built on wooden piles. They have saddleback roofs whose gables sweep up at an even more exaggerated pitch than those of the Toba Batak. Traditionally, the roof is constructed with layered bamboo, and the wooden structure of the house assembled in tongue-and-groove fashion without nails. Nowadays, of course, zinc roofs and nails are used increasingly.

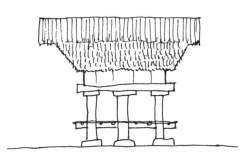

The construction of a traditional *rumah adat* is time-consuming and complex, and requires the employment of skilled craftsmen. First of all, seasoned timber is collected, then a shed of bamboo scaffolding with a bamboo shingle roof is erected. Here, components of the house are prefabricated, though the final assembly will take place at the actual site. Almost invariably now, *tongkonan* are raised on vertical piles rather than on a substructure of the log-cabin type, so all the wooden piles are shaped and mortises cut in them to take the horizontal tie beams. The piles are notched at the top to accommodate the longitudinal and transverse beams of the upper structure. The substructure is then assembled at the final site. Next, the transverse beams are fitted into the piles, then notched and the longitudinal beams set into them, and the grooved uprights that will form the frame for the side walls are pegged in place. Thin side panels are cut to the dimensions decided on by the woodcarver who is going to decorate them, and slotted in. The two outermost uprights of each transverse wall pass through the upper horizontal wall beam and, being forked at the upper end, carry the parallel horizontal beams that support the rafters. A narrow hardwood post, also forked at the top and set into the central longitudinal floor beam, runs up each transverse wall, is anchored to the upper wall beam and carries the ridge purlin. The rafters are laid over the ridge purlin, whose extended ends rest on the triangular overhanging gables. An upper ridge pole is then laid in the crosses formed by the rafters, and the ridge pole and ridge purlin lashed together with rattan.

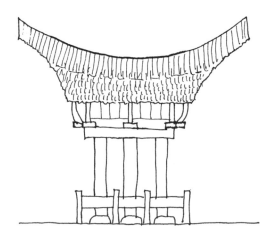

To obtain the increasingly curved roof so popular with the Toraja, the ends of the upper ridge pole must be slotted through the centres of short vertical hanging

Opposite *Roof structures of Toraja rice barns, set on a log-cabin base* (above), *and raised on pillars* (centre and below).

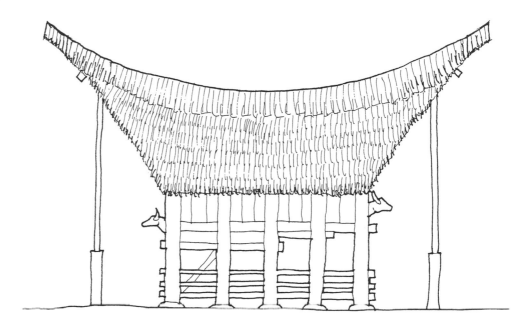

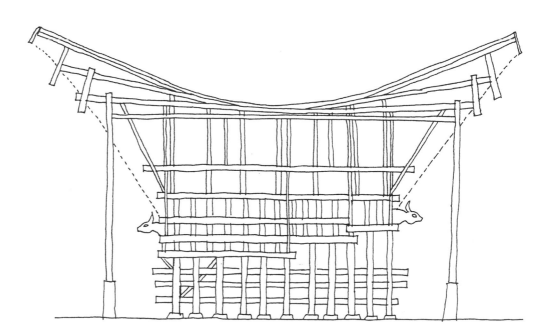

Side view and longitudinal section of a Toraja tongkonan.

spars, whose upper halves support the first of the upwardly angled beams at the front and rear of the house, which in turn slots through the centre of further short vertical hanging spars that carry the second upwardly angled beam. The sections of the ridge pole projecting beyond the ridge purlin are supported front and back by a freestanding pole. Transverse ties pass through both the hanging spars and the freestanding posts to support the rafters of the projecting roof. Before the roof is fitted, stones are placed under the piles. The roof is made of bamboo staves bound together with rattan and assembled transversely in layers over an under-roof of bamboo poles, which are tied longitudinally to the rafters. Flooring is of wooden boards laid over thin hardwood joists.

A new *tongkonan* at Pa'tengko, just outside Makale, took eight men three months to build, and six men one month to carve and paint the outside wall panels. There is no carving inside recently built Toraja houses, but on occasion timbers from old houses are reused in the construction of new ones. In Bintu Lepang, in the Solo district of Tana Toraja, there is a house which dates from about 1950 that was made out of beams and posts from three older houses. Here old carved exterior beams were incorporated into the new interior. This *tongkonan* was notorious for housing an unburied corpse from 1964 until 1992, as a result of a dispute between the dead woman's adopted children. The body was soaked in coffee to preserve it and wrapped in over fifty of her textiles to smother the smell and to stop the heirs from squabbling over the them. The government finally had to order the funeral to take place.

Toraja society is extremely hierarchical, comprising nobility, commoners and a lower class who were formerly slaves. Villagers are only permitted to adorn their house with the symbols and motifs appropriate to their social station. The gables and the wooden wall panels are incised with geometric, spiralling designs and motifs such as buffalo heads and cockerels painted in red, white, yellow and black, the colours that represent the various festivals of Aluk To Dolo ('the Way of the Ancestors'), the indigenous Toraja religion. Black symbolizes death and darkness; yellow, God's blessing and power; white, the colour of flesh and bone, means purity; and red, the colour of blood, symbolizes human life. The pigments used were of readily available materials, soot for black, lime for white and coloured earth for red and yellow; *tuak* (palm wine) was used to strengthen the colours. The artists who decorated the house were traditionally paid with buffalo. The majority of the carvings on Toraja houses and granaries signify prosperity and fertility, and the motifs used are those important to the owner's family. Circular motifs represent the sun, the symbol of power, a golden *kris* (knife) symbolizes wealth and buffalo heads stand for prosperity and ritual sacrifice. Many of the designs are associated with water, which in itself symbolizes life, fertility and prolific rice fields. Tadpoles and water-weeds, both of which breed rapidly, represent hopes for many children.

Opposite **88** *A sacrificial buffalo in the padi fields in front of the ancestral village of Buntu Lepong, Tana Toraja, southern Sulawesi.*

The Toraja *live in the isolated mountainous regions of south Sulawesi. Although over half the Toraja are Christian, they have retained many customs associated with their old animist faith, including animal sacrifice, ostentatious funeral rites and huge communal feasts. They build magnificent traditional houses raised on stilts.*
89 *A buffalo head made from painted wood and buffalo-dung, but crowned with real horns, mounted on a house facade in Sa'dan village. The panelling is incised with patterns of spirals, stars and buffalo heads painted in black, red and white.*
90 *A body lying in state, wrapped in fine batik textiles, in a house of the dead in Tana Toraja.* **91** *Three ancestral houses of origin, known as* banua Toraja, *or* tongkonan. *Two have high upswept roof peaks made of bamboo shingles protected by sheets of zinc; the other, more humble roof is thatched. All three roof projections are supported by an external wooden pillar.* **92** *A child sits by the platform of a rice barn in Tana Toraja. The barn is decorated with designs of buffalo heads with outstretched horns.* **93** *The interior of a tongkonan is cramped and dark, having few windows. The under-roofing is of bamboo culm.*

90 △

◁89

91 △

92 △

93 △

95 △

The Toraja tongkonan *is the focus of family identity and tradition, and represents all the descendants of a founding ancestor.* **94** A tongkonan *under construction near Makale, surrounded by bamboo scaffolding lashed together with rattan. The carved and painted gable is decorated with symbolic motifs of buffalo heads, suns, cockerels and spirals.*
95 Tongkonan, *rice barns and modern Bugis-style houses seen through a bamboo grove.* **96** *Frames in the shape of* tongkonan *used to carry coffins, resting by a cliff-face burial area. Each mausoleum is sealed off by a carved and painted door.*
97 *A rice barn, with a decaying bamboo shingle roof protected by a sheet of zinc, faces low, old-style, thatched* tongkonan. *Rice stooks are left to dry outside.*
Overleaf **98** *The open platform of a rice barn opposite two traditionally thatched* tongkonan *is frequently used as a meeting place and recreation area.*

96 △

97 △

99 △   101 ▽   102 ▽   100 △   103 ▽

Tongkonan *are built on wooden piles, and are put together with pegs and wedges rather than with nails. Their saddleback roofs with dramatically upswept gables are constructed with layered bamboo.*
99 *Rice stooks drying in front of* tongkonan. *In the background is a contemporary Bugis-style house. Light and well ventilated, it is the kind of house in which most modern Toraja will now live.*
100 *From the platform of a rice barn, the bamboo construction of a* tongkonan *roof can be seen.* **101** *A vertical array of sacrificial buffalo horns adorning the support post of a house. The facade is composed of carved and painted panels and the roof is made of bamboo culms and shingles.* **102, 103** *A church, made of light wall panels of split and flattened interwoven bamboo. The church bell is a wheel hub from an old truck.* **104** *Buffalo-head and scroll patterns on the decorative panels of a* tongkonan *at Kete Kesu village, Tana Toraja.* **105** *Children sitting on the open platform of a rice barn. Its wall panels have been carved and painted with scroll and buffalo-head patterns.*

104 △

105 △

107 △

The seafaring Bugis are to be found all over the Indonesian archipelago. For years the Bugis have lived in pile-built wooden houses with slatted bamboo floors, similar in style and layout to the basic Malay prototype. Their buildings are usually decorated with crossed roof finials symbolizing buffalo horns. **106** The hearth and cooking implements of a house in Talkalar village. The walls and floor are made from simple planking. **107** A family on the steps of a contemporary pile-built house crowned with the traditional crossed finials. The house has many windows to ensure good ventilation in the warm, moist climate. **108–10** Within the wooden planking walls of a Bugis home, such modern appurtenances as a television and a sewing machine can be found. The roof is of zinc, and the windows have louvred shutters.

108 △

109 △

110 △

123

Bugis buildings share the symbolic architectural divisions found all over the archipelago. The shaded recess underneath the house, a depository for rubbish and a stall for animals, corresponds to the underworld; the raised living quarters represent the human world; and the attic space where the family heirlooms are stored is symbolic of the upperworld. The house is regarded as a spiritual entity, whose most important architectural feature, its central pillar, is known as the posi bola, *the navel, vital centre and source of power of the house.* **111** *A house in Maros, southern Sulawesi, raised on wooden piles, with part of the undercroft walled off with wooden planking.*
112 *The undercroft of another house at Maros is fenced in with bamboo, providing a storage area or animal shelter.*
113–18 *The crossed finials that surmount Bugis gables may vary in size and shape, but all represent buffalo horns.*

111 △

112 △

113 △

114 △

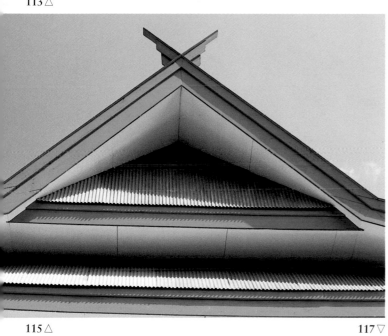
115 △

116 △

117 ▽

118 ▽

121 △

122 △

The island of Borneo is divided into Kalimantan, which is Indonesian, the Malaysian states of Sarawak and Sabah, and the sultanate of Brunei. Its indigenous peoples are the Dayaks, whose most characteristic form of housing is the longhouse. **119** A Dayak longhouse in Kalimantan, constructed with hardwood piles and main beams.
120 The verandah of a Dayak longhouse is a communal area used for meetings, craftwork, dancing, rice-pounding and recreation. **121** A painted house of the Pawan Dayak, who live in the Ketapang area of Kalimantan. **122** A grave painting and wooden roof tiles of a charnel house in the middle Mahakam River area of Kalimantan. Dayak cemeteries, or 'villages of the dead', vary from earth burial mounds to 'villages' of decorative charnel houses. **123** A brightly painted panel of a Kenyah Dayak meeting hall, featuring a central human figure surrounded by motifs of hornbill and dragon spirits. In Kenyah cosmology, the hornbill is a messenger from the supreme god of the upperworld.

123 △

127

124 △

125 △

Dayak villages are found on the banks of the vast meandering rivers of the interior. Mancong is a Benuaq Dayak village in the lower Mahakam River area. Its oldest longhouse dates back to the 1870s.
124 Protective carved wooden spirit figures outside the old two-storey longhouse.
125 A carved step-log, surmounted by a protective spirit figure. **126** The loadbearing hardwood pillars and beams of the longhouse undercroft. **127** Decorative woodwork on the longhouse verandah.
128 The gallery of the longhouse. The doorways and windows belong to separate family apartments.
Overleaf **129** Tiered verandahs of the old longhouse at Mancong. Carved hardwood protective spirits guard the stairways.

126 △

127 △

128 ▷

Longhouses can provide shelter for just a few families, or can house an entire village. Though each family in the longhouse can retire to its own private quarters, all but the most personal activities take place on the communal verandah, a shaded gallery that runs along the whole length of the longhouse. At night the gallery provides a sleeping place for guests and the young men of the tribe. In former times the severed, preserved heads of enemies used to be hung from the rafters of the verandah as protective talismans. The longhouse verandah is the social focus of the whole community. Whole trunks of ironwood are used for the piles and beams of Borneo longhouses and are often used again for building anew, after an old building has been abandoned. **130** The interior of a Benuaq Dayak longhouse at Tanjung Isuy. Abaca fibre ikat hangings line the walls. **131** The shingles that clad the roof of this Benuaq Dayak longhouse are of ironwood. **132** Children playing outside a longhouse at Tanjung Isuy. **133, 134** Tree bark is used to make the wall panels of this longhouse, and carved protective spirits guard the stairways.

130 △

131 △

132 △

133 ▽

134 ▽

135△   136▽   137▽

138 △

The longhouse verandah plays a crucial role in the life of the community, and is protected by carvings of guardian spirits. It is the place for village meetings and ceremonies, and many of these rituals focus on the finely carved step-log, which is the only collectively owned object in the longhouse. **135** Carved guardian figures and step-logs outside two longhouses at Tanjung Isuy. **136** Propped against a balcony is a step-log, with a copulating couple carved at the top. A man at prayer is carved on the balcony post and a spirit effigy protects the step-log. **137** A carved guardian figure, outside a covered porchway with painted eaves, clad with ironwood shingles. **138** Simple single-family houses by the Mahakam River. **139** A woman squatting in front of her clapboard house by the Mahakam River.

139 △

Opposite **140** *A carved hardwood longhouse wall panel with a painted border and bas-relief carving of Aso, the dog-god figure, and* naga *dragons, combined in the fantastical swirling style of the Kenyah Dayaks of central Kalimantan.*

Many of the motifs that adorn the houses and granaries of the Toraja are identical to those found on the bronze kettle drums of the Dong-Son. Others, such as the square cross motif, are thought to have Hindu-Buddhist origins or to have been copied from Indian trade cloths. The cross is used by the Christian Toraja as a decorative design emblematic of their faith. On the front wall of the most important houses of origin is mounted a realistically carved wooden buffalo head, adorned with actual horns. This emblem may only be added to the house after one of the most important funeral rites has been celebrated.

Village layout varies according to size. As a general rule, in the larger settlements of Tana Toraja the houses are arranged in a row, side by side, with their front gables facing north. Each house stands opposite its own rice barn, and together these form a complementary row parallel to the houses. Roofs are aligned on a north-south axis. Houses of the Mamasa Toraja are not orientated in this way but follow the direction of the river, and their rice barns are set at right-angles to the houses. The major agricultural ceremonies of the Toraja year are celebrated in the area between the houses and the barns.

To the Toraja, the *tongkonan* is more than just a structure. The symbol of family identity and tradition, representing all the descendants of a founding ancestor, it is the focus of ritual life. It forms the most important nexus within the web of kinship. Torajans may have difficulty defining their exact relationship to distant kin, but can always name the natal houses of parents, grandparents and sometimes distant ancestors, for they consider themselves to be related through these houses. Descent amongst the Toraja is traced bilaterally – that is, through both the male and female line. People therefore belong to more than one house. Membership of these houses only requires the kinsman's active participation at times of ceremony, the division of an inheritance or when a house is rebuilt.

Although the *tongkonan* has become identified by outsiders as being representative of all Toraja building, it is only the nobility and their descendants who can afford both the building of the houses themselves and the enormous ritual feasts associated with them. Noble Toraja can claim affiliation to a particular *tongkonan* as descendants of the founding ancestor, through the male or female line. This association is periodically confirmed through contributions to the ceremonial feasts given by the *tongkonan* household. Commoners customarily lived in smaller, simpler houses and acted as helpers at these communal feasts. Commoners trace their descent through their own houses of origin. These, although of simpler design and decoration, may still be known as *tongkonan*.

Upon marriage, Toraja men will usually go to live with their wives. If they later divorce, the husband is the one who will leave, his ex-wife being left in possession of a house that he may have spent much time, energy and money on refurbishing. He is often compensated by being given the rice barn, which he

dismantles and removes. The *tongkonan* is never moved. One important reason for this is that a large number of placentae are buried to the east side of the house (east is associated with life in Toraja mythology). The placentae, buried by the fathers of new-born children, are believed to call them back if in their adult life they ever journey a long way from home, so ensuring that they will always return to their house of origin.

As in so many places in modern Indonesia, the traditional house, with its cramped, dark, smoky interior, has lost its attraction for many Toraja (although it still commands great ritual prestige). Many have opted for a ground-built, concrete, single-storey house in the contemporary Pan-Indonesian style, and some have adopted a wooden, pile-built Bugis-type dwelling. Others who are more inclined towards tradition may add an extra storey and a saddleback roof; this provides more living space and room for furniture whilst retaining something of the prestige the *tongkonan* affords its owner.

The seafaring Bugis are to be found all over the Indonesian archipelago. They have settled in the Riau Islands, Sumatra, Kalimantan, Sumbawa and Malaysia, and they trade in all the smaller islands. There are records of the Bugis collecting *trepang* (sea-slugs) in the Gulf of Carpentaria long before the discovery of Australia by the Europeans.

The Bugis have traditionally lived in pile-built wooden houses with slatted bamboo floors similar in style and layout to the basic Malay prototype. The characteristic decorative feature is a pair of crossed roof finials symbolizing buffalo horns. In her book *The Living House*, the anthropologist Roxana Waterson details three archaic architectural styles differentiated by their roof line, which is either straight, convex or saddleback. Nearly all old Bugis buildings were

Above, left *A painted panel depicting buffalo heads on the front of a Toraja rice barn and* (above) *a stylized representation of a branch of moss on a Toraja tongkonan.*

destroyed in the political troubles of the 1950s when they were regarded as relics of the pre-Islamic, pagan past. Present Bugis buildings have a straight ridge line, but retain the divisions in function and the cosmic symbolism that is common to all the pile-built dwellings of the archipelago. The shaded recess underneath the house, a depository for rubbish and a stall for livestock, corresponds to the underworld; the raised living quarters above is the human realm; and the roofed-over attic space where the family heirlooms are stored is symbolic of the upper-world. The house is conceived of as both a spiritual and a corporeal entity whose most important architectural feature, its central pillar, is known as the *posi bola*, the navel, the house's vital centre and source of power.

The people of Minahasa, Sulawesi's northern peninsula, are closely related to ethnic groups of the neighbouring southern Philippines. Long Christianized and subject to colonial influence, the Minahasans were for many years the most literate people in Indonesia. Minahasa is densely populated, prosperous and intensively farmed.

Before the days of Dutch colonization, the Minahasans and neighbouring groups lived in great houses that were shared between several families. Built of wood and thatch, they were raised on thick wooden pillars and had steeply pitched roofs. Family apartments, with their own cooking and rice-storage facilities, were usually grouped around a central communal room. What is now regarded as a traditional Minahasan house only developed in the nineteenth century, and is yet another variant of the Malay house, raised on tall piles, with a steeply pitched gambrel roof. The gables are decorated in floral patterns with painted wooden beading. The house is entered by means of twin stairways either side of a spacious, shaded front verandah.

The traditional houses of the rugged and isolated peninsula of south-east Sulawesi utilize the timber from its still-extensive forests. Raised on piles, with many windows and shaded verandahs at the front and back, the richer houses rise in tiers with the gabled roof of the upper storey set upon the truncated gabled roof of the lower.

Central Sulawesi, lying to the north of the Toraja lands, is even more isolated. There the *rumah adat* have very tall, steeply pitched roofs with gables that are inclined slightly inwards. The buildings are raised on massive, crudely hewn hardwood piles. Roofs are covered either with hardwood shingles or with thatch.

The great island of Borneo, the third largest in the world, straddles the equator. Erosion and volcanic activity have moulded its terrain. The central mountain range culminating in the northern peak of Mount Kinabalu is the highest chain between the Himalayas and New Guinea. Large alluvial plains lie between lesser mountains, and the great rivers such as the Kapuas, the Mahakam and the Barito-Kahayan meander through the plains forming ox-bows and wide, shallow lakes eventually reaching the sea via large marshy deltas, into which they deposit vast amounts of silt and clay. As the interior of the island is covered with virgin rain forest (the largest outside Amazonia), roads are almost nonexistent and the rivers form the main arteries of communication.

Borneo is divided politically between the countries of Malaysia, Brunei and Indonesia. The Malaysian states of Sarawak and Sabah and the kingdom of Brunei occupy the north-western and northern parts of the island; the remainder, which takes up approximately three quarters of the land area, is Indonesian and is known as Kalimantan. The total population of Borneo is around seven million, with five-and-a-half million living in Kalimantan.

Borneo, abundantly rich in raw materials and forest products, has always been subject to foreign influence, as it lies on the trade routes between China, the Philippines and Java. The coastal towns of Sarawak, Brunei and Sabah have strong Malay and Chinese components, and the littoral settlements of Kalimantan are dominated by Bugis, Banjars, Javanese and Chinese. The Chinese have dominated trade throughout the whole of South-East Asia, and have traded with Borneo for many centuries. There was much Chinese immigration, initially motivated by work in the rich mines of the island. The archetypal style of Bornean housing, the longhouse raised on stilts, bears striking similarities to traditional Chinese bazaar architecture; this has led to speculation as to whether the longhouse is an indigenous type or a product of Chinese influence.

The indigenous people, known to the outside world as the Dayaks, inhabit villages set up on the banks of the vast meandering rivers of the interior. Living by shifting rice cultivation and by the farming of sago palms, they are divided by tribes which were formerly prone to the internecine warfare that their head-hunting customs demanded. Although now they are mostly converted to Christianity, their cultures retain a great deal of their original vigour. Those Dayaks who have converted to Islam style themselves 'Melayu' (Malay) to distinguish themselves from non-Islamic Dayaks. There has been much intermarriage between the Dayaks and other racial groups, particularly in the towns.

Traditionally, the Dayaks live in communal longhouses. Known as *lamin* in east and west Kalimantan, Sarawak and Brunei, they are one room deep, set on piles and often up to 300 metres (975 ft) long. In southern and central Kalimantan they are laid out differently, to a rectangular and sometimes even square plan, and are known as *balai* and *betang* respectively.

A group of longhouses or a single very large longhouse makes up the traditional village. The piles can be up to 3 metres (nearly 10 ft) tall. At this height, the longhouses catch the cooling upper breezes, avoid the majority of the ground-hugging mosquitoes and are protected from marauding wild animals and raiding parties of hostile tribes. Access to the various sections of the longhouse is by way of stairs made from a notched log that can, if necessary, be drawn up. Pigs and chickens can also be kept in pens underneath the house.

The longhouses are divided internally, so that each family has its own separate living quarters which it owns, along with the corresponding section of the verandah that runs right down one of the long sides of the house, or centrally between two parallel rows of living quarters. The verandah is shared communally, however, and plays a crucial role in the life of the longhouse community. It not only acts as the main thoroughfare and provides a shaded work area for domestic tasks, but is also the venue for village meetings and for the performance of ceremonies that are considered vital to the spiritual and material well-being of the community. Many of these rituals focus on the finely carved stairway log, which is the only collectively owned object in the longhouse.

Longhouses are always built in such a way that they can be easily dismantled and transported to a fresh location: traditionally, the Dayaks would practise slash-and-burn cultivation, which rapidly exhausts the thin layer of tropical top soil and requires constant migration to fresh sites.

Rainfall in Borneo is among the highest in the world. The mean annual rainfall at Kuching is over 4 metres (13 ft). This immense amount of rain has produced, in the lowlands, a hugely tall forest of an incredible variety of *Dipterocarp* trees. Even when these forest giants are felled, a lower, more open, secondary forest quickly grows to replace them. Mangrove trees fill the coastal swamps and everywhere in the lowlands is to be found a wide variety of species of bamboo, rattan and various palms. Traditional housing styles vary between the different indigenous ethnic groups, and indeed, not all of them live in villages. The Punan are nomadic forest-dwellers who live in temporary leaf-and-bough shelters deep in what remains of the virgin forest.

Of the Dayak tribes, the Iban (sometimes known as the Sea-Dayaks) are the most well known to the Western world. Famously aggressive and land-hungry, they dominate the Malaysian state of Sarawak, forming nearly a third of the population. Coming originally from west Borneo, where some isolated groups remain, they live in communal longhouses and customarily practise slash-and-burn dry-rice cultivation. Iban society is relatively egalitarian but extremely competitive. In the past they were much-feared head-hunters.

In his book *Hornbill and Dragon*, the anthropologist Bernard Sellato lists the tribes of Borneo. These include the other prominent Dayak grouping in Sarawak, found in the west of the state, the Land Dayaks, who comprise the Bidayuh, the Kendayan and the Selako; these peoples also live in longhouses, and have a relatively unstructured social organization. Villages are grouped around a central circular meeting hall, where heads taken in battle were once exhibited. Women are not allowed here. The Dusun, the Murut, the Bajau, the Tidong, the Bulungan and the Bisayah, who live in the northern state of Sabah, neighbouring areas of Brunei and east Kalimantan, are related and belong to the same language group as the peoples of Mindanao and the Sulu Islands in the Philippines. Most of these groups live in isolated longhouses. The Dusun also had special houses for displaying heads.

The Kayan and the Kenyah of central Borneo occupy the upper reaches of the great rivers. Once famous for their head-hunting and slave-taking, they are now dry-rice farmers. They produce some of the most fantastic art in the whole of tribal South-East Asia; renowned as excellent blacksmiths, they craft the much-prized *mandau* swords. Kayan villages consist of a single, large longhouse. The Kenyah, who may be the descendants of forest nomads, live in large villages of up to five thousand people. The village population is spread out between several longhouses, each ruled over by the presiding aristocrat. Their longhouses are adorned with emblems denoting status; the symbols of the aristocracy ornament the long galleries. Smaller tribal groups such as the Maloh and the Taman of the upper Kapuas and the Aoheng on the Mahakam have adopted the social structure of the Kayan and its central feature, the Kayan longhouse.

The Kelabit, the Lun Dayeh and the Lun Bawang, living in the north-east, and the Berawan and the Kajang in Sarawak are all peoples that have for many years been impinged upon by Muslim groups pressing in from the coast and the war-like Kayan and the Kenyah from the centre. This has largely resulted in their assimilation into one or other of these dominant groups, as the smaller tribes have gradually adopted their social practices and architectural styles.

The Barito people are the most numerous in all Borneo, and are to be found throughout southern Kalimantan. They include the Ngaju, the Ot Danum, the Siang, the Murung, the Luangan, the Ma'anyan, the Benuaq, Bentian and the Tunjung. These groups are noted for their fine wood carving, basketry and mat-weaving, and are renowned for their elaborate death rituals. They live in villages that are not highly structured, and some of them have never built longhouses. The Ngaju and related groups build large houses known as *uma hai*, which are shared by an extended family but do not shelter unrelated families as a true long-house would.

Although the Melayu consider themselves Malay and often claim Sumatran, Malayan or even Arab descent, they are in fact ethnic Dayaks, albeit now converted to the Islamic faith. Inhabiting the coastal regions and the banks of the major rivers, they have adopted the Malay way of life, and occupy single-family wooden houses, set on piles, with the typical Malay verandah. A popular alternative to the pile-built house is a modest single-storey construction set on a floating pontoon.

The Punan, the forest nomads and the most archetypal of all Borneo's inhabitants, are gentle, shy hunters and gatherers living in the deep virgin rain forest of central Borneo. Their way of life is threatened by the huge scale of commercial logging operations, particularly on the Malaysian side of the border. Punan houses are rudimentary lean-tos, easy to erect and dismantle. As they are made

An Iban Dayak floral motif carved on a doorpost in Sarawak.

from leaf and bough, they are naturally camouflaged to help protect their inhabitants from other predatory tribes.

Longhouses can provide shelter for just a few families or else can house a whole village. Only a few of Borneo's Dayak tribes erect purely public buildings, as the longhouse of most tribes serves as both a public and private domain, and is the social focus of the community. Although each family in the longhouse can retire to its own private quarters with cooking and sleeping areas and storage facilities for rice and family heirlooms, all but the most personal activities take place on the communal verandah, a shaded gallery that runs along the whole length of the longhouse. It is here that meetings are held, ceremonies are conducted, women plait baskets, mend nets and clean rice; children play here, and longhouse members of all ages converse. At night, the gallery provides a sleeping place for guests and the young men of the tribe. In former times the severed, preserved heads of enemies used to be hung from the rafters of the verandah as protective talismans.

A Kenyah Dayak mural featuring spiralling dragons.

Although in other parts of the archipelago teak and *cengal* are used to make piles, in the forests of Borneo there was until recent times an abundance of ironwood. Whole trunks of ironwood are used to make the piles and beams of Bornean longhouses, and these are often re-used once an old building has been abandoned. Until the late nineteenth century, longhouses were often built on huge piles, some as tall as 12 metres (40 ft). This not only lifted the inhabitants well above the night-time malarial mosquitoes and the stinking rubbish that accumulated beneath, but also acted as a defensive measure against other raiding tribes. The only way to penetrate such a longhouse after the log stairs had been drawn up would have been to attempt to cut or burn down the supporting piles. Methods of construction and materials used differ from tribe to tribe, depending on social structure, the degree of permanency required, and the availability of raw materials. The leaf-and-bough shelters of the Punan nomads are the most basic, and although they were sometimes occupied for long periods, they could be constructed or dismantled in less than a day. There is no architectural ornamentation to these dwellings or any social differentiation between them.

The relatively egalitarian Iban were dependent for their livelihood on slash-and-burn dry-rice cultivation, which meant that they periodically moved village when they had exhausted the fertility of one area and required fresh land. Light wood, bamboo, bark and even leaves were commonly used building materials, as they could be easily and quickly worked and did not require the arduous and time-consuming labour necessary with hardwoods. Piles were not that tall and often only consisted of light poles.

An Iban village commonly consists of a single longhouse, or *rumah*, divided into *bilek* (family apartments) opening out onto a *tanju* (a shaded gallery). Several families will share the longhouse and see themselves as a coherent community, but each is responsible for making its own decisions. Though Iban society contains rich, important and influential lineages, the Iban do not divide themselves up by social class. Each family builds its own unit within the longhouse with whatever materials are preferred. Consequently, the overall appearance of an Iban longhouse would often be rather ramshackle and seem not very solidly built.

At the opposite extreme, the Kayan and Kenyah are sedentary societies able to expend time and much effort in the construction of beautifully crafted longhouses designed to last for generations. Though the Kenyah and the Kayan are traditional enemies, there are sociological similarities between the two tribes that are reflected in their architecture. In both societies, longhouses are called *uma* and are built on ironwood pillars to raise them high above the ground. They use other hardwoods for floors and walls, and the roofs are made of ironwood shingles tough enough to withstand the torrential monsoon rains. Posts and beams are lashed together with rattan. The single longhouse that comprises the Kayan village consists of many family apartments known as *amin*. Both Kayan and Kenyah houses testify to highly sophisticated joinery skills and are adorned with much intricate woodcarving and painting. Even the steps cut into the ironwood log that functions as a stairway are embellished with carved demonic faces intended to frighten away threatening evil spirits.

The layout of the longhouses reflects the hierarchical structure of these communities. Kayan society was stratified into *maren* (aristocrats), *hipuy* (nobles), *panyin* (commoners) and *dipen* (slaves), and Kenyah society was similar in structure. In the longhouses of both tribes, the interior apartments were allocated strictly according to social status. The largest living quarters belonged to the chief, the ruling aristocrat, and were located centrally for security, flanked by the apartments of other nobles, and with their roof raised to a slightly higher level than the rest of the longhouse. Now, in more peaceful times, the chief's quarters may be at the end of the longhouse, so that they can be easily extended. All the nobles and most especially the chief will decorate their quarters with a profusion of special motifs indicating their status. Prominent among these is Aso, the dog-god, whose image functions both as the badge of aristocracy and as an anthropomorphic ancestor figure. The apartment of the ruler of a Kenyah longhouse is decorated with a huge mural, whilst outside in the communal gallery trophy heads are hung above ritual drums and other sacred objects.

A carved wooden sculpture, home of Bali Akang, the god of bravery, is imbedded in the ground outside the Kenyah longhouse. The family living areas for commoners are traditionally found either side of the nobles' apartments, and the slaves were quartered at the extreme ends of the longhouse, in the places most vulnerable to attack. A longhouse may contain up to thirty apartments in all.

An Aso motif painted on the wall of a Kenyah Dayak meeting hall.

Longhouses are usually built parallel to the river, and rice barns and store-houses containing valuables will be situated beside the main building, set apart in case of fire, which is a common hazard. The kitchen is also sometimes separate. The concentration of the whole village into two or three longhouses was stategically advantageous, and ensured an economic use of structural timber. Longhouses are between 60 metres (200 ft) to 150 metres (500 ft) long; the local terrain can rarely accommodate a larger structure. The long gallery that faces the river used to be protected by a wooden lattice grill that prevented enemy raiders hurling projectiles into it. Kenyah and Kayan longhouses have fantastically carved and painted finials and murals, depicting Aso and Burong, and other important figures connected with the spirit world. Another feature of Kayan and Kenyah architecture is their funerary structures – the *kelirieng*, a burial pole, and the *salong*, a burial hut. The *kelirieng* is an enormous carved hardwood tree trunk inset with niches to contain the bodies of slaughtered slaves. A jar containing the bones of a chief is set into the top of the trunk and covered with a heavy stone slab. The *salong* is a wooden chamber containing jars full of aristocrats' bones supported by one or more poles. The outside of the chamber is painted with spiralling Aso figures and other designs, and fretted and painted wooden friezes and corner projections of the same motifs provide additional decoration.

The only social distinction made by the Ngaju of southern Kalimantan was between *utu*, free men, and slaves. It is doubtful that they ever built longhouses – they live in pile-built wooden single-family houses. The Banjars of Banjarmasin are a mixture of immigrant Javanese and native Dayak blood. Their traditional houses are built in the Malay style with a gabled roof that diminishes in pitch at about ceiling height and extends out on both sides more shallowly. The houses stand on wooden piles 4.6 metres (15 ft) high, and their gable walls are carved and painted with bas-relief floral and vegetal designs. Roofs are tiled with wooden tongue-shaped shingles and have ornate crossed buffalo-horn wooden finials. A wooden stairway at the side affords access to the house.

As in most other parts of the archipelago, the numbers of people living in traditional houses in Borneo is in steep decline. Christian and Islamic opinion perceives the communal life of the longhouse as both unhygienic and morally subversive. Government attitudes, particularly on the Indonesian side of the border, have encouraged both migration out of traditional living areas and the abandonment of traditional longhouses. The seductions of the modern world have also taken their toll; air-conditioned videoboats are now a common sight on the rivers of Sarawak. The voracious logging industry all over Borneo also lures tribesmen away from their home villages and starts to detribalize them, encouraging them to move into single-family dwellings and abandon their traditional architecture. Carpentry and woodcarving skills, however, are still in great demand for boat and house building, and for making tourist artefacts, and the government, becoming increasingly aware of the potential of the tourist industry, is now just beginning to reverse its former policy and actively encourage Dayaks to remain in their longhouses.

5
The
Outer Islands

THE OUTER ISLANDS to the east of Bali are populated by peoples who, with certain significant exceptions, have only been converted to either Christianity or Islam in the recent past. Despite their new espousal of different faiths, they share certain common cultural traits, which are still to be found unadulterated by the trappings of the world religions in Sumba, Irian Jaya and in some of the isolated islands of the southern Moluccas. The outer islanders have great reverence for the spirits of their ancestors, hold ostentatious funerals and have only recently abandoned the traditions of intervillage and intertribal warfare that were once so common all over the archipelago. Although the architectural traditions of Irian Jaya, the eastern, Indonesian half of New Guinea, are related to the housing styles of neighbouring Indonesian islands, the west Irians' basically stone-age culture has much more in common with that of Melanesia and Micronesia.

The ancestral house of origin, from the vast communal pile-built houses once found amongst the Manggarai of west Flores, to the beehive-roofed houses of the Atoni in Timor and the great hat-shaped houses of Sumba, is of central importance to all these islanders. Even though the villagers may now live in houses built in the contemporary Javanese style, the traditional *rumah adat* is the central focus of a villager's life.

Nusa Tenggara, the chain of islands that stretches east of Bali, loses its tropical lushness in eastern Lombok and becomes progressively more arid through Sumbawa, Flores, Sumba and Timor. The climate, which is hot and dry, is greatly affected by the islands' proximity to the enormous desert continent of Australia. Peopled by races of mixed Malay and Melanesian origin, the islands were divided up into a great many principalities, often at war with each other and prone to domination from whichever external power could exert influence upon them; they have owed allegiance to the Javanese, Balinese, Makassarese and Bugis, the Portuguese and the Dutch. Sometimes these powers established settlements on the outer islands – the Balinese in Lombok, the Makassarese and Bugis in Bima, the Dutch in Kupang and Rote and the Portuguese in Flores and east Timor; but mainly they paid tribute as and when necessary, traded sandalwood, spices and slaves, and conducted their internecine wars.

Although the climate is arid, timber has until recently been in plentiful supply, and bamboo, rattan, and sugar, sago, coconut and *lontar* palms grow in most locations, ensuring a ready supply of building materials. Eastern Nusa Tenggara is not in general a rice-growing area; agricultural production is provided by slash-and-burn cultivation, and nowadays the staple crop is maize. Wet-rice culti-vation, with its need for the maximum amount of uninterrupted land, encour-ages the concentration of houses into compact villages, but in the outer islands maize is grown in patches close to houses, and given that population density and the amount of water available to sustain that population are both low, houses are generally spread out in small groups. Though ancestral villages, ruled over by hereditary princes or their descendants, consist of houses grouped around the cultural focus of a cluster of *rumah adat*, the majority of houses are now spread out in scattered hamlets across the countryside.

Timor is a long, narrow island. A central mountain chain runs its length, and it is crossed with wide stony river beds. The Atoni, the original inhabitants, occupy most of the western half of the island. The main centres of Atoni settle-ment are around Mount Mutis and the towns of So'e and Kefamenanu. The Belu or Tetum, supposedly of Malay origin, are more recent interlopers, arriving in the fourteenth century to colonize the centre of Timor. To the east live, amongst others, the Mambai tribe.

For centuries, west Timor was ruled by the Dutch; it then became an integral part of newly independent Indonesia. East Timor, ruled by the Portuguese until 1975, enjoyed hardly a year of independence before it was unilaterally annexed by Indonesia, leading to a brutal war and insurrection that continues to this day. The Atoni were encouraged by the Dutch – as part of their ethical policy – to abandon their traditional haystack-shaped dwellings and to move into ridge-roofed houses. The Atoni have now mainly adopted this type of housing, but have constructed these new buildings beside their old homes, which are used as kitchens and, very importantly, as storage places for dried corn cobs.

A pattern carved on the pillar of an Atoni rice barn in west Timor.

A carved wooden panel of birds and horses on a Belu house, west Timor.

The traditional haystack-style dwelling is very simply made: a circle of vertical bamboo poles are bent into a central point, bound and tensioned by horizontal rings of bamboo, which are tied together with lengths of palm leaf, rattan or shards of bamboo at intervals of a foot or so. The lattice thus formed is thatched with sheaves of *alang-alang* grass, which are tied on in layers starting from the bottom rung up to the top. The thatch almost reaches the ground, but is trimmed at the bottom to form a neat edge. The weight of the roof is partially borne on a massive wooden frame. This consists of four stout pillars set into the packed earth floor, which bear the weight of two large beams. These in turn support six beams laid over them, surmounted by four more positioned across these. The projecting ends of this network of beams support one of the roof rings about halfway down. The main function of this massive box frame, however, is to take the weight of a great number of dried maize corn cobs, which are stacked on and suspended from it over the ever-smouldering hearth that lies beneath. The larger 'haystack' structures have a circular wall of flattened bamboo.

Most Atoni now live in the modern variant of the traditional house. This has a hipped roof, a wooden post-and-lintel frame, and wall sections made up of coconut-palm leaf spines. The structural frame consists of six posts, set either into the ground or into a laterite pediment, which support a ring beam, and are braced by wooden roof girders. The roof, thatched with *alang-alang* grass, rests on the ridge, supported by king posts.

The pride of the Atoni who live around Kefamenanu is the *lopo* granary (a 'haystack' on wooden piers) which can be up to 7.6 metres (25 ft) to over 9 metres (30 ft) in diameter. The barn space is enclosed within the roof, which is supported on four posts approximately 2.8 metres (9 ft) high, that are topped with a square section of tree trunk to keep out rats. As with the Atoni 'haystack' house, these pillars support two heavy beams, on which are laid a cross-lattice of beams. These in turn support a ring of the roof frame. The eaves of the roof overhang this beam by 1.2 metres (4 ft).

The floor of the granary is of opened-out, flattened bamboo. Entry into the granary roof space is through a single wooden trap door, which is often beautifully carved. Thatch is again of *alang-alang* grass, tied to split bamboo purlins with *ijuk* cord and either shards of bamboo or palm-leaf. The shady undercroft of the *lopo* is for social and recreational use, and for weaving, which constitutes a woman's main occupation.

In the Insana area, *lopo* have a short ridge topping the barn roof. Various methods are used to reinforce the thatch at this crucial point in order to keep it waterproof and the grainstore dry. An extra layer of *alang-alang* thatch is added, and held down with coconut branches, a section of hollow tree trunk or even a piece of zinc roofing. The *alang-alang* grass is often plaited along the top of the ridge, and is teased up into two horn-like finials sticking up about 45 centimetres

(18 in.) from each end. These finials can be elaborated into shapes and figures: a man and a woman, the head or tail of a cow or horse, or perhaps just a simple cross.

Between Kefamenanu and Belu province, many of the more modern houses will have a medium-sized *lopo* and an elliptical *rumah adat*. The *rumah adat* is not lived in but is used to store heirlooms. The old rajah's house at Maslete near Kefamenanu is elliptical in plan, with a ridged roof 4.6 metres (15 ft) long and up to approximately 9 metres (30 ft) high, thatched with *alang-alang*. The front third of the house is a verandah shaded by the roof, which is here supported by six external pillars. Three stout wooden pillars directly support the ridge. Pole rafters lead down to a wall of wooden planks, which is about 1.5 metres (5ft) high. This, with the aid of external poles, takes the weight of the roof. The roof is extended over the verandah with the aid of additional rafters, whose interior ends are carved in the shape of cockerel heads. The whole house is raised on a stone podium.

The traditional housing of the Belu people around Betun in central Timor consists of gable-roofed, wood and thatch houses raised on small wooden pillars. The houses are orientated on a north-south axis, with a shaded porch on the north face. The roof ridge is supported directly by two wooden pillars and the floor is of slatted bamboo. At the south end of the house is a set of open cubicles in three sections. The side portions are for food and cooking pots, and the central one contains the actual hearth. This structure also helps to support the roof. The adults sleep in the inner part of the house, children on the verandah, which is used during the day for socializing and for weaving. In certain Belu villages the external house walls are decorated with beautifully painted mats.

The tall, *ijuk*-thatched, stilted *rumah adat* of Los Palos, far to the east of Timor, are known as *uma lautem*. Built of teak wood and raised on painted hardwood piles, their roof ridges are bedecked with strands of cowrie and nautilus shells, which hang down from the ridge pole.

The economy of Rote, the southernmost of all the Indonesian islands, is based on cattle-raising and toddy-tapping. It exports to the nearby city of Kupang in Timor. Traditional houses in Rote had a ridge roof with *lontar* palm thatch that came down nearly to the ground with crossed buffalo-horn finials made of wood, a single door and no windows. They were dismissed by the Dutch anthropologist Van de Wetering in 1923 as unworthy even of the name 'haystack', and most of the surviving examples were demolished by the local administration in the 1970s on the grounds that they were unhygienic. Rote is now highly Christianized.

The isle of Flores lies to the west of Timor and to the north of Sumba. Named 'Cape of Flowers' ('Capa da Flores') by the first Portuguese to arrive, in 1512, it is an astoundingly beautiful island of wooded valleys and soft hills inhabited by people of mixed Malay and Melanesian descent. A source of sandalwood and

A wooden door of the Belu people of central Timor, carved with geometric patterning and breast-shapes.

slaves, Flores was also long the focus of first Portuguese and then Dutch missionary endeavour. The island is now predominantly Catholic, particularly in the Sikka district which centres around Maumere on the north coast; there are some strong Muslim enclaves, however, such as Ende on the south coast, which have resulted from centuries of Bugis and Makassarese influence. The Florinese are agriculturists. Their main crop is maize but recently they have embarked on wet-rice cultivation. The lush valleys abound with coconut, sugar and *lontar* palms, deciduous trees and tall stands of bamboo that can grow to a great girth.

In the hills of the Lio district, on the slopes of Mount Kelimutu, local construction is overwhelmingly of bamboo. The richer houses have thatched, gabled roofs, and a hardwood and coconut-wood post-and-lintel structural frame set on a stone and cement plinth foundation. Ceilings and inner partitions are of split bamboo. Wall panels are of interwoven split bamboo and are nailed to the timber frame. Windows are of interlaced openwork split bamboo.

Flowers, stars and diamonds, geometric motifs and crouching human figures are some of the forms and images that are used to decorate the wall panels of Lio houses. The patterning is created by contrasting the outer and inner surfaces of the stripped bamboo, and after the natural colour of the bamboo has faded, the outer strips of bamboo are painted white to accentuate the contrast with the natural bamboo colour of the inner strips.

The poorer people live in post-and-lintel huts where most, if not all, of the loadbearing elements are bamboo posts. Wall panels are of interwoven bamboo splints or opened, flattened bamboo sections. Roofs are thatched with *alang-alang* grass or are laid with interlocking half-rounds of bamboo or bamboo shingles. Gables are merely air vents formed by bamboo posts roughly covered with dried coconut leaf.

The light, sturdy and flexible nature of bamboo structures is extremely important in areas prone to earthquake and hurricane. The havoc wreaked by the tidal wave and earthquake that hit Maumere in late 1992, for instance, is still evident many miles inland, and it is the reinforced concrete buildings rather than the traditional structures that have been irreparably damaged. The 150-year-old *rumah adat* at Wolawaru survived unscathed, whilst all the neighbouring reinforced concrete structures were completely destroyed.

The *rumah adat* of the Lio district are still in evidence, though not abundant, raised on low wooden pillars and crowned with the same high-hat roof as their Sumbanese counterparts, but not built to the same vast dimensions. The roof is supported by a system of two or three concentric rectangular ring beams resting on pillars that increase in height the nearer they are to the centre. The high-hat extension is provided by a cantilever ridge beam built on to a supporting beam across the centre of the inner ring beam, and can be braced by diagonal beams.

The grid of low wooden pillars upon which the house stands is made of coconut-palm stumps which rest on stone plinths to protect them from rot and allow movement during earthquakes. Wall panels are of planed jakwood planking, floors of whole culms of bamboo and inner partitions and non-loadbearing outer walls of interwoven split bamboo or coconut matting. Kitchens are now usually found at the rear or to either side of the house rather than around a central hearth. The front quarter of the roof overhangs a verandah which runs the full width of the house. A raised platform of bamboo culms on bamboo posts about one metre (3 ft) high is built flush with the rear of the house. The most important houses are entered by way of a wooden staircase that leads up to a beautifully carved doorway, with bas-relief carved jambs and lintels in the shape of elongated cockerels or boats, incorporating fish, gun and floral motifs, and central figures of crouching males and females. Traditional villages are laid out in two parallel rows of houses facing each other, with an open central area containing megaliths, tombs and now a grotto to the Virgin Mary.

West Flores is one of the most beautiful areas in Indonesia. The terrain is rugged, but fertile clumps of bamboo, sugar and coconut palm, bananas, jak and breadfruit trees, and coffee, cocoa and teak plantations abound in the narrow valleys between the soft-edged hills, and the dormant volcanoes beyond. In the wider valleys grow maize, vegetables, manioc and sweet potato, and also a little wet rice.

To the far west are found the Manggarai people, centred around Ruteng, who were ruled for an extended period by the Makassarese dynasty of Bima in Sumbawa. The Manggarai once lived in great communal houses which were either conical or elliptical in plan, built on very low piles with a roof of *alang-alang* thatch that almost reached the ground. These houses were not only home to many families, they were also the focus of the *adat*, the ceremonies of the native religion.

The vast Manggarai houses were demolished at the instigation of both Catholic missionaries and Dutch health officials, who were concerned by the appalling incidence of hookworm, lung diseases and dysentery caused by the gloomy smoke-filled interiors and middens filled with excrement that lay beneath the slatted floors. From the 1930s on, after a brief and unsuccessful experimentation with square-plan housing, the Manggarai began living in single-family groups, in smaller conical-roofed houses. They also now live in Javanese-style bungalows.

Just to the east of the Manggarai lies the Ngada country. The Ngada and related groups were the last people in Flores to be brought into contact with the white colonizers and their Westernizing influences. Consequently, the native religion is still a cultural force of some importance. Each village is arranged around the male and female totems belonging to each clan.

Opposite **141** *A traditional Atoni house in the So'e district of west Timor. Atoni houses are thatched with* alang-alang *grass and look like haystacks. The Atoni now use these structures as kitchens and for storing and drying maize, and live in timber-framed houses.*

The pride of the Atoni who live around Kefamenanu in west Timor is the lopo granary, which can measure from 7.5 to 9 metres (25 to 30 ft) in diameter, and is supported on four stout wooden posts, surmounted by a section of tree trunk to act as protection against rats. The shady undercroft of the lopo is for recreational use, and for weaving (a woman's main occupation). **142** A lopo and outbuilding in the compound of the regent's house in Maslete, west Timor. **143** A conical Atoni house thatched with alang-alang grass, now used as a kitchen, in the So'e district. **144** The underview of a lopo at Maslete. Alang-alang thatch is bound to the roof frame and trimmed neatly around the bottom edge. A post-and-beam structure supports the roof and the barn space, the floor of which is constructed out of split and flattened bamboo. The top of the pillar is fitted with a wooden disc to prevent rats from entering. **145** The carved and painted post of a rice barn at Maslete. The same designs are used in Atoni tattoos and in the ikat textiles of the region. **146** The men of a hamlet near Kefa helping to thatch a rice barn with alang-alang grass.

145 △

146 △

147 *The regent's house at Maslete seen from beneath its enormous and most prestigious rice barn. The platform to the right of the house, which rests on the fork of an old tree, was once used to display severed heads. It now bears offerings of sheep skulls and maize cobs.* **148** *The interior of traditional Atoni hut, near So'e. Stout supporting pillars not only carry the weight of the roof but in addition an enormous quantity of dried maize cobs, which are stored above the hearth.*
149 *Atoni women, sitting between a new-style timber-framed house and an old 'haystack' model, trim and finish weavings.*

148 △

149 △

◁147

150 △

151 △

152 △

153 △

150 *Roof finials in the shape of a cow's head and tail, teased up from the alang-alang* thatch *of the ridge roof on an Atoni house near Insana, in west Timor.*
151 *Carved wooden figures of hens and birds on the wooden cover for the ridge roll of a regent's house in the Kefa district of Timor.* 152 *Decorative finials on the ridge roll of an Atoni house in west Timor.*
153 *A carved dancing human figure on a door of a wooden house in a Belu village in central Timor.* 154 *Smoke filtering through the thatched roof of a traditional Atoni house. The smoke helps to preserve the thatch.* 155 *An old house frame ready for refurbishing, in the So'e district of west Timor.* 156 *A stylized crocodile figure and geometric patterning on a Belu door.*

154 △

155 ▽ 156 ▽

The Ngada and the peoples related to them were the last in Flores to be brought into contact with the white colonizers and their westernizing influences. Village houses are grouped around the male and female totems belonging to each clan. The ngadhu, *the male totem, is a pole 3 metres (10 ft) high, on top of which is an umbrella of thatch surmounted by a phallus-shape of whipped* ijuk *cord, with arms, holding a* parang *and a spear. The female totem, the* bhaga, *is a house-like shrine – a thatched wooden box open on one side, set on wooden posts. Bena, near Bajawa in the west, is one of the most traditional Ngada villages, and its stone monuments are protected.* 157 *Bena rises up in plazas containing* ngadhu *and* bhaga *male and female totems, flanked by a row of houses on each side. A male figure made out of* ijuk *cord adorns the nearest roof ridge.*
158 *Buffalo horns taken from buffalo slaughtered for sacrificial feasts are displayed at the corner of a traditional house.* 159 *A* ngadhu *and* bhaga.
160 *A grandmother with her grandchild, preparing sirih. The verandah where they sit has a carved and painted border.*
161 *A pillar, beamwork, half-culm bamboo flooring and pegged tenon and mortise joints.*

158 △

◁157

159 △

160 △

161 △

162 △

163 △

164 ▽

165 △

The class divisions within Ngada society are still quite strict. Although men of the upper class can marry whom they please, lower-class men can only marry into their own class. Social divisions are made apparent by means of a miniature house that is fixed on the thatched ridge of an upper-class house. A lower-class house can be identified by a male figure with parang and spear on its roof. **162** A male figure made of wood and ijuk fibre and armed with spear and parang, marking the roof ridge of a commoner's house in Bena. **163** Commoners' houses, crowned with armed male figures. The roofs of the verandahs are clad with interlocking half-culms of bamboo. **164** A row of parasol-shaped ngadhu in a village near Bajawa. **165** A skilled carpenter and his assistant stop work on a house in Bena for tea and sirih. The house has beautifully carved and painted lintels, and wall panels of jakfruit wood. **166** A Bena carpenter making a tenon and mortise joint between a coconut wood beam and a bamboo post.

166 △

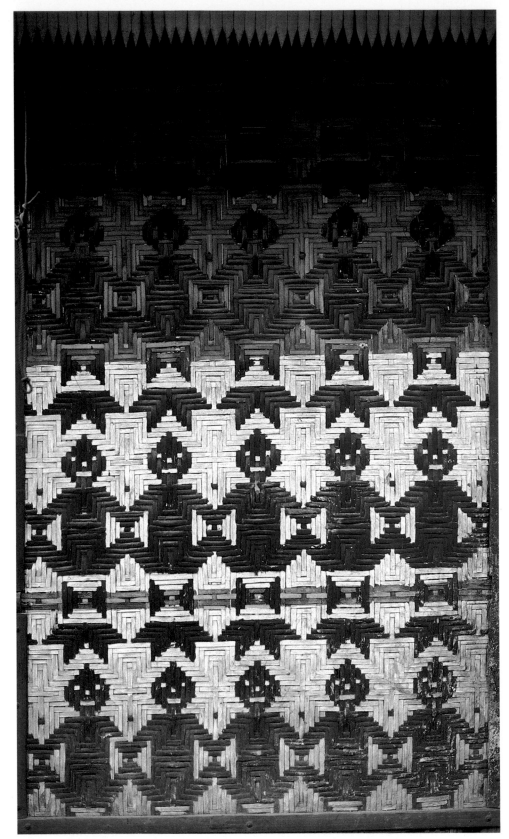

In the hills of the Lio district of Flores, on the slopes of Mount Kelimutu, most local construction is of bamboo. The distinctive decorative feature of Lio building is the geometric patterning and crouching human figures in the wall panels, which are made by contrasting the dull inner side of the split bamboo with the shiny outer surface. After the natural colour of the bamboo has faded, the pattern is painted on.

167 Designs of human figures painted in blue and white on the wall panels of a building above Wolowaru. **168** Rumah adat in Wolowaru, with lontar palms growing close by. **169** A house in the rice fields at Wolowaru. The house is thatched with alang-alang grass and painted patterns of human figures adorn the interwoven split bamboo wall panels. **170** Rolls of geometrically patterned interwoven bamboo ready for use as wall panelling. **171** Villagers remove the chaff from rice grains outside a recently built house, set on a concrete and stone plinth, with newly woven wall panels.

167 △

168 △

169△ 170▽ 171▽

172 △

173 ▽ 174 ▽

Sumba lies to the south of Flores and to the west of Savu and Timor. It is renowned for its Pasola festivals – mock battles between teams of horsemen – and its glorious ikat textiles. It is divided culturally and geographically into east and west. The east is a dry savannah and famous horse-raising area, and though more sparsely populated, was always politically dominant. The west is hilly, even mountainous. The west was divided into many warring fiefdoms.

172 Pigs among stone graves on the central plaza of Tarung village in west Sumba, surrounded by rumah adat with 'high-hat' roofs. **173** Rumah adat in Tarung, with timber for building lying ready for use. **174** A dog sleeping on a stone tomb, in front of a newly constructed rumah adat, freshly thatched with alang-alang grass, in Tarung. **175** A couple preparing sirih in the doorway of an enormous rumah adat in Pau village, east Sumba. **176** Timbers laid out for joint-cutting. **177** Peeled manioc roots drying on a stone tomb in Pasunga village. On the top slab of the tomb a human figure is carved. In the background stands a rumah adat with a surrounding bamboo verandah typical of west Sumba.

175 ▽

176 △

177 △

The Sumbanese rumah adat, *with its distinctive 'high hat' thatched roof, is found all over the island with the same basic structure. The adat roofs in the far west of Sumba are the highest. A verandah a few steps lower than the floor of the house is set into the front and rear, and is reserved for weaving and socializing.*
178 *The wall panels of two east Sumbanese houses are made up of spines of coconut leaf (left) and of interwoven split bamboo.* **179** *The verandah of a* rumah adat *at Rende, east Sumba, with great horns and skulls of sacrificed male buffalo below the door jambs.* **180** *Wood and bamboo have been used in the construction of this* rumah adat *in Tarung. The roof is thatched with* alang-alang *grass.*

178 △

179 △

180 ▷

The layout of a Sumbanese village is based on two parallel rows of houses facing each other across an open space containing table-like tombstones and carved limestone megaliths. All houses are raised on 1.5 metre (5 ft) piles, so there is plenty of space to keep animals and poultry below. **181** The construction of a 'high-hat' roof of a new rumah adat *in Tarung. Bamboo culms, rafters and purlins are used extensively.* **182, 183** *Zoomorphic male and female figures, and horses with* sirih *bowls (symbols of bravery and hospitality) carved on memorial stones in Pasunga, west Sumba.* **184** *Memorial figures on the graves of two past rajas, in Kawangu, east Sumba, with the raja's house in the background. The figures wear the Dutch hats that were a badge of office.* **185** *Old carved hardwood house pillars have been reused in the construction of a new* rumah adat.

181 △

182 △

183 △

184 △   185 ▽

186 △

187 △

Irian Jaya is the western, Indonesian, half of the enormous island of New Guinea. One of the most ethnographically interesting areas is the Baliem valley in the central highlands. Isolated from contact with the coast by some of the most rugged terrain on earth, the valley was first revealed to the world by a pioneering explorer and aviator, Richard Archbold, in 1938, who discovered the Dani, the predominant local tribe. Though equipped only with stone-age tools, the Dani's building and agricultural techniques were surprisingly sophisticated. Surrounded by their well-tilled fields of young taro, sweet potato and other vegetables, the Dani live in small family compounds, each well defended with its own stockade.

186 The cooking hut in a compound near Wamena. The stones in the right foreground can be heated in a fire and then placed in a pit to cook pigmeat and taro for feasts. 187 A Dani elder wearing a penis gourd outside the men's hut in the Wamena district of the Baliem valley. Vegetable gardens lie behind a protective stockade. Dani architecture is characteristically defensive because of their unbroken history of sporadic tribal warfare. 188 A Dani girl, daubed with decorative markings and wearing a fibre skirt, sits in the doorway of a woman's hut in the Wamena district.

A typical Dani compound consists of a long cooking shed, and four to six circular huts known as honay, *with thatched dome-shaped roofs. At the far end of the compound is the men's hut where the adult and adolescent males sleep, and where talismanic relics are kept.* **189** *The gateway, stile and stockade at the entrance to a Dani family compound near Wamena. To defend the compound, the doorway can be easily blocked off and barred with two stout planks.* **190** *In this Dani compound near Kurima, the cooking hut is to the left, the men's hut in the distance, and women's huts to the right.* **191** *Dani tribesmen socializing on the shaded bench beside the men's hut in a compound near Jiwika in the Baliem valley. A mummified male ancestor is kept in this hut.*

189 △

190 △

191 ▷

The *ngadhu,* the male totem pole, is 3 metres (10 ft) high, topped with an umbrella of *alang-alang* thatch and surmounted by a phallic shape made of whipped *ijuk* cord and equipped with arms of *ijuk* fibre that hold a *parang* and a spear. The female totem, the *bhaga,* is a house-like shrine, a thatched wooden box open on one side supported on wooden posts. Both *ngadhu* and *bhaga* are set on dry stone plinths. When a clan builds a new house, a buffalo is sacrificed near the *nghadu,* and clan members will initiate certain important feasts around the *ngadhu, bhaga* and surrounding megaliths before retreating to their own houses to complete the feast.

Houses in Ngada villages are arranged in parallel rows facing each other, with *ngadhu* and *bhaga* belonging to the various clans arranged between them. On flat ground they will be assembled in a neat row, but in a village on a steep slope, such as Bena, near Bajawa, the totems and megaliths are set into plazas, each with its own dry stone walls, which rise in tiers to the highest point of the village. In Bena this is occupied by a grotto to the Virgin Mary and a *ngadhu*-shaped parasol shading a bench from which the stupendous view can be admired. The Ngada see no conflict in this juxtaposition of Christian and animist symbols.

Ngada houses are raised on low timber piles. These support a grid of squared-off coconut beams, on which rests a floor of flattened bamboo. The coconut wood beams are mortised into each other and secured with wedges. Decorative panels painted with motifs – flowers, foliage, horses – flank the floor beams (the pillars rest on stone plinths to deter rot and offer more flexibility during earth tremors). On top of the floor frame is laid a ring beam of grooved coconut, into which are slotted jakwood or teak planks fitted side by side, flush with each other. Another ring beam of grooved coconut slots on top of the wood panels. Two interior rooms are built in this fashion, and the roof frame of stripped bough and bamboo rafters springs up from this ring beam. The roof frame is the same high-hat or hipped model found in the Lio district or in Sumba and is supported in the same manner; it is thatched with *alang-alang* grass tied with rattan or *ijuk* fibre to bamboo purlins. A front verandah built on low timber piles with a bamboo roof and timber panelling runs right across the front of the house. This shaded area is occupied mainly by women who weave and chew *sirih* there. The front and side walls are studded with vertically arranged horns of sacrificed buffalo. The verandah is reached by centrally located wooden steps. The entrance to the house is rarely decorated, but the doorway from the first interior room to the rear room is adorned at its top with crude but dramatic incised carvings depicting foliage, buffalo horns, horses, cockerels and textile patterns. The bottom and lower sides of the doorway are carved in the shape of steps which are said to symbolize the steps that have to be followed in order to contact ancestors. The rear room of the house is divided by woven split bamboo panels into a central area, with a kitchen on one side and storage area on the other.

Wooden panel carved in bas-relief in the inner sanctuary of a Ngada ancestral home in central Flores.

The class divisions within Ngada society are still quite strict. Men of the upper class are allowed to marry women of their own or the lower class, but others are only permitted to marry into their own class. Class divisions are made apparent by means of a miniature house that is placed on the thatched ridge of an upper-class home, or by the male figure with *parang* and spear that denotes lower-class occupants.

The extra thatch on the roof ridge is held on with split bamboo battens, tied on with *ijuk* cord. Vents made up of tied rolls of *alang-alang* grass are set into the sides of the roof ridges to allow the smoke from the central hearth to escape. Spear and *parang*-like bamboo splints radiate from each ridge end, and a ceiling of bamboo provides attic space for storing heirlooms and other valuables.

Sumbawa, situated between Lombok and Flores, is divided culturally and geographically into two distinct halves. The west is subject to Balinese influence, the east to that of the Bugis. On the western side of the island and in Bima in the east, houses are raised on stilts and are thatched with *alang-alang* grass. Bima is noted for its rice granaries known as *lengge*. The Donggo people inhabit the mountains of Bima, and live in single-room 'A'-framed houses with high thatched roofs, though the coming of Islam has brought many social changes and the abandonment of most traditional housing. Most of the Bimanese and the people of west Sumbawa now live in contemporary ground-built Javanese-style dwellings.

Sumba, lying to the south of Flores and to the west of Savu and Timor, is an island famous for its beautiful horses, its Pasola festivals, and the wonderful ikat textiles that are made there. It is divided culturally and geographically into east

A mamuli ornament carved on a memorial stone in east Sumba.

and west. In the east lies the dry horse-raising savannah, but the west is hilly, even mountainous, with kapok, teak, bamboo and coconut and sugar palms growing in the valleys. The Sumbanese survive on a sparse diet of maize and manioc supplemented by fish and the occasional meat feast of pig and buffalo. For centuries, the west has been divided by warring fiefdoms. The east, though more sparsely populated, has always been politically dominant.

The Sumbanese *rumah adat*, with its distinctive high-hat thatched roof (looking rather like an English Civil War Puritan's hat) is to be found all over the island. Its basic framework consists of two or three concentric rectangles of squared-off timber posts, each supporting a ring beam and each taller than the last. The central, highest, ring beam is laid over with three cross beams. The central cross beam supports an 'n'-shaped ridge which creates the conventional hipped-roof shape. The high-hat extension is achieved by raising the 'n'-shaped ridge and giving it a number of simple horizontal cross-beam supports, or creating a stripped bough trestle, which springs up from a platform built on top of the central ring beam, and then laying bamboo rafters on it. The *adat* houses to the far west of Sumba have the tallest high hats. Walls are of interwoven split bamboo nailed on with battens, or of interwoven coconut-leaf panels, or sometimes coconut leaf ribs threaded horizontally onto vertically set bamboo spikes. Floors are of whole bamboo culms. A verandah a foot or so lower than the floor level of the rest of the house is set into the front and rear, and is reserved for weaving and recreation. Traditionally, all interior timbers are tied together with rattan. Thatch is of *alang-alang* grass tied on to stripped bough battens with coconut leaf. The extra layer of thatch at the top is surmounted with vertical wooden finials representing human figures, and riders on horseback.

The village layout comprises two parallel rows of houses facing each other across an open space containing table-like tombstones and carved limestone megaliths. All Sumbanese houses are raised on piles about 1.5 metres (5 ft) high, so there is plenty of space below to keep animals and poultry. They have a verandah which runs right across the front face of the house; verandahs in the verdant west are floored with whole bamboo, which is more abundant than in the east, and they have a raised L-shaped bamboo bench at each corner. The eaves in western Sumba overhang open storage space on each side and at the rear, whereas in the east, roofs descend to meet the walls.

Irian Jaya is the western, Indonesian, half of the enormous island of New Guinea, bounded by rocky inlets on its northern coast and an enormous tidal swamp on its southern littoral. One of the most ethnographically interesting areas is the Baliem valley in the central highlands. Isolated from contact with the coast by some of the most rugged terrain on earth, the valley was first revealed to the world by a pioneering explorer and aviator, Richard Archbold, in 1938. He discovered the Dani, the predominant local tribe, whose men were clad only in penis gourds, and the women in grass skirts. Despite being equipped with stone-age tools, the Dani's agricultural practices, bridge-building and domestic architecture were surprisingly sophisticated.

The broad valley can still only be reached by air, and when the aeroplane descends below the clouds that top the mountains, it appears as a maze of interlocking elliptical agricultural plots, each surrounded by its own irrigation and drainage ditches, with clusters of thatched huts that comprise a group of several conical huts adjacent to one longer building.

Dani architecture has evolved to suit the needs of a society dominated by agriculture, pig-rearing and ritualized warfare. Unusually in New Guinea, where slash-and-burn cultivation is the norm, the Dani practise settled agriculture, in the Baliem valley. The valley may once have contained a lake, and is now a long, wide flood plain fed by sediment brought down by the Baliem river from its sources on Mount Trikora.

Surrounded by their well-tilled fields of taro, sweet potato and other vegetables, the Dani live in small family compounds, each well defended with its own stockade, made of a double row of sharpened pine stakes with lateral bars of the same, tied in with rattan. At head height, approximately one foot below the pointed tips of the stakes, lengths of brushwood are laid transversely across the top of the fence and then covered with leaves, ferns and moss, presumably to absorb the almost daily rainfall and to stop the fence from rotting in the absence of preservatives. Entrance to the compound is through a styled gateway that can be shut off with two stout planks.

A typical compound can house up to four related men and their families (approximately twenty people in all), under the direction of an acknowledged dominant male. Accommodation within the compound is provided by four to six circular huts known as *honay,* surmounted by a thatched dome-shaped haystack roof descending to within one metre (3 ft) of the ground. At the far end of the compound is the men's hut, in which sleep the adult and adolescent males, and in which such talismanic relics as the smoked and blackened, mummified body of a long-dead ancestor are stored. The interior is approximately 4.6 metres (15 ft) in diameter, the floor of raised earth strewn with straw, and the pine stakes that form the exterior wall are lined with bark or interwoven split cane to exclude draughts.

The huts are designed to retain heat during the night hours, and embers are kept continually smouldering in the central hearth. This is formed by four tall upright poles driven into the ground in a square pattern and given additional support and stability by cross beams tied in approximately one metre above the packed earth floor. These four vertical poles reach up to the central point of the roof and, along with the circular wall of pine stakes, bear its weight. The roof is composed of a closely fitted lattice of stripped tree boughs springing up from the top of the wall to the central point of the cone, and is trussed laterally with bamboo purlins tied together with rattan. The roof trellis is covered with thatch of *alang-alang* grass. Smoke from the hearth is an important factor in the preservation of the thatch; otherwise, in such a wet climate, it would rot after a couple of months. The flat, low ceilings are made of closely spaced cane laid over bamboo culms, which are tied into the wall stakes to roof over the living space. The hut walls, like the compound fencing, are formed from a double row of pine stakes enclosing short lengths of pine planking tied in with lengths of rattan. The entrance to the hut is through a small doorway equipped with a stout lockable door made out of a single piece of wood. Further protection is given by a row of stake fencing in front of the walls that flank the doorway. *Honay* take about three days to construct, a day to build the wooden framework, a day to thatch the roof and a day to complete the interior. All the men of the compound work on the new building and are assisted by the women and children.

Although Christian missionary activity has left its mark on the Dani, they are still predominantly polygamous, and the women take on most of the burden of agricultural labour and other work. The women's huts are smaller versions of the men's. Each hut houses one woman and her children. Men and women lead segregated lives. Children are breastfed till seven years of age, and the women abstain from sex for two to six years after the baby is born. The women's huts lie along one side of the compound each joined to the other by a stockade of double pine stakes. This stockade joins the women's quarters to the men's at one end and to the front fence of the compound at the other. The men's hut is flanked on both sides by a shelter with a lean-to roof, which covers a bench on which men or women can sit and converse. Most of the other side of the compound is taken up by a long cooking shed, with a gabled roof. The interior contains three or four working hearths, and at one end there are usually pens for pigs, which are bred for festival times.

The cooking hut is approximately 15 to 20 metres (50 to 65 ft) long, with a ridge-beam supported by five to seven central poles driven into the ground. The roof frame is made up of wooden pole rafters and bamboo purlins, over which a thatch of *alang-alang* grass is made. Extra support is given by six or seven vertical poles driven into the ground approximately one foot from each longitudinal wall.

The layout of a Dani compound is overwhelmingly defensive in character. Outbreaks of the endemic intervillage warfare occur sporadically and unpredictably. The outer stockade will not only enclose the inner courtyard, surrounded by living and cooking huts, but also small vegetable gardens, pig-pens and exterior cooking areas (pits of stones that are heated up to cook the vast pigmeat and sweet potato feasts eaten at festival times). As an additional measure, each compound is aligned with others belonging to allied families to form an easily defensible village. Indonesian government policy towards the Dani has in most cases been reasonably tolerant. At one stage, the government tried to get the Dani to wear clothes, and there was also a misguided attempt to lure them away from their traditional *honay* and into zinc-roofed shacks. The shacks were too hot during the day, however, and too cold at night.

The Yali are a tribe who live in the hills. Their huts resemble those of the Dani, except that they are thatched with palm instead of *alang-alang*. Another tribe, the Asmat, live on the Causarina coast in the southern coastal swamps. Most of their traditional forms of housing have been destroyed on government orders over the last twenty years. Traditionally, they were fearsome head-hunters. They lived in villages on bends in the river, which offered the best vantage points from which to spot the approach of hostile canoe-borne raiding parties. Villages accommodated several clans and were large enough to provide an adequate defensive force. Each clan maintained a large men's house known as a *jew*.

Raised on short piles and facing the river, these houses were up to 90 metres (300 ft) long and consisted of a framework of timber posts lashed together with palm leaf. The wall panels were made of palm-leaf battens. A long shaded veran-dah ran the length of the house. There were many doors set into the verandah wall, each leading to a fire pit by the back wall. In some areas only bachelors lived in the *jew*. Family houses were located between the various *jew* on tall piles or even in trees. Though these houses were the focus of religious and social life, they were destroyed on government orders in 1964. Some *jew* survive far up river, but the vast majority of the Asmat now live in family huts in a radically changed cultural and economic environment. Their lands are being heavily logged, and the government has expended a great amount of time and effort on eradicating their indigenous culture.

The southern part of Biak Island, off the north coast of Irian Jaya, is known for its spirit-houses, which have steepled roofs thatched with *ijuk* palm fibre some 18.5 metres (60 ft) tall, known as *karuwari*. These have now long fallen into disuse.

The Moluccas, the original spice islands, stretch from the north of Halma-hera to Tanimbar and beyond, in the far south-east. *Rumah adat* in Tanimbar are raised on wooden pillars about 1.5 metres (5 ft) high. They have thatched roofs whose ridges sometimes project beyond the slightly inwardly inclined gables, and are crowned with crossed wooden buffalo-horn finials, but they have no windows. The houses are clustered around a boat-shaped plaza that was once used for ceremonial sacrifice and other rituals.

On the Babar islands along the south-west Irian coast, boats also feature in village iconography. The great houses that once existed on Dawela and Dawelor islands were orientated in the direction of a sailing boat voyaging from sunrise to sunset. The rooms were given names that accorded with their position on this sailing boat, the helmsman's part being in the east and the pilot's in the west. Inside the house people would sit with their backs to the eastern part of the house. Right would correspond to north, left to south. The rooms in the eastern part of the house were known as the helmsman's cooking area, flanked by the helmsman's right-hand and left-hand room. To the west were the corresponding pilot's rooms and in between was an open area known as the *ottuwlesol*, where guests were entertained, all the men would eat, and the bachelors among them sleep.

The outer islands are still little affected by the baleful acculturizing influences of the industrialized world. Tourism is still very much in its infancy and cannot be said to have had any real effect on the islanders' culture as yet. Some traditional housing forms – the great communal houses, for instance – have vanished already, the victims of missionary interference and government paternalism; others are now decrepit. The Indonesian government has for many years broken the power of the local rajas, and though the ex-rulers still have much social prestige, the hierarchy of which they are the pinnacle has lost much of its force and capacity to generate wealth. The future of the *rumah adat* in these islands is limited, and the influence of Christian and Muslim missionaries will further diminish their role. At most, they will possibly be rebuilt as tourist attractions in the traditional *adat* villages, but with the onslaught of the television age, it is unlikely that the islanders will seek to live in them in the future.

Carved wooden tavu *(house altar) from Tanimbar, south-east Moluccas.*

Glossary

adat custom and tradition

alaman street area separating houses from their rice granaries, in the villages of the Toba Batak (Sumatra)

alang-alang common type of grass, used for thatching

Aluk To Dolo traditional religion of the Toraja (Sulawesi)

amin family apartments of a Kayan Dayak longhouse (Borneo)

Angkola Batak group (Sumatra)

Asmat indigenous group (Irian Jaya)

atap thatch

Atoni indigenous group (Timor)

Badui indigenous group (Java)

balai Dayak longhouse laid out to a rectangular plan (Borneo)

bale public meeting hall, or private pavilion

banjar residential part of a Balinese village

banua Toraja house (Sulawesi)

Barito indigenous group (Borneo)

Belu indigenous group (Timor)

betang Dayak longhouse laid out to a square plan

bhaga female totem of the Ngada (Flores)

bilek family apartments of an Iban Dayak longhouse (Borneo)

bomoh a spirit medium

Bugis seafaring group from Sulawesi, found throughout the archipelago

Burong mythical bird

candi Hindu temple found in Java and Bali

cili depictions of Dewi Sri, the rice goddess (Bali)

dalem the rear of a Javanese house, containing the *sentong*

Dani indigenous group (Irian Jaya)

Dayak indigenous group (Borneo)

Donggo indigenous group (Sumbawa)

enau sugar palm

geriten Karo Batak ossuary (Sumatra)

honay circular hut of the Dani (Irian Jaya)

ijuk the black fibre that clings to the trunk of the sugar palm, a popular thatching material

jabu Toba Batak traditional house (Sumatra)

jew Asmat men's house (Irian Jaya)

kabong sugar palm

kadiofe rectangular, pile-built meeting hall (Enggano)

kaja upstream, or 'towards the mountain' (Bali)

kampung a village compound

kangin east (Bali)

karang stylized carvings of protective demons (Bali)

Karo Batak group (Sumatra)

karuwari spirit house (Biak)

kauh west (Bali)

Kayan Dayak group (Borneo)

kepala desa village chief

kelirieng Kenyah and Kayan Dayak burial pole (Borneo)

kelod downstream, or 'towards the sea' (Bali)

Kenyah Dayak group (Borneo)

kuren a Balinese home

labe labe longitudinal beam of a Toba Batak *jabu* (Sumatra)

lalep a single-storey family house (Mentawai)

lamin Dayak communal longhouse (Borneo)

lengge rice granary, Bima (Sumbawa)

lesung rice-pounding house, Karo Batak (Sumatra)

lontar the palmyra palm

lopo Atoni granary (Timor)

lumbung Balinese granary; Sasak bonnet-roofed granary (Lombok)

Makassarese indigenous group (Sulawesi)

Mamasa Toraja group (Sulawesi)

mamuli vulva-shaped ornament (Sumba)

Mandailing Batak group (Sumatra)

Manggarai indigenous group (Flores)

Melayu Muslims of Malay or claiming Malay descent (Borneo)

merantau Minangkabau custom whereby men will travel far from their villages to earn money, only returning at periodic intervals

mussalah house for adolescent males, Minangkabau (Sumatra)

Ngada indigenous group (Flores)

ngadhu male totem of the Ngada (Flores)

Ngaju Barito group (Borneo)

naga mythical snake- or dragon-like creature

nua traditional house, Lampung (Sumatra)

omo sebua the chief's house in the villages of south Nias

orang asli the ancient peoples of Indonesia, who occupy the interiors of the main islands and most of the outlying islands

Ot Danum Barito group (Borneo)

Pakpak Batak group (Sumatra)

paon Balinese kitchen

parang machete

paras soft sandstone (Bali)

Pasola festival consisting of a mock cavalry battle (Sumba)

pekarangan compound of a Balinese house

pendopo large open pavilion for the reception of guests (Java)

posi bola central pillar of a Bugis house

prahu sailing vessel

pringgitan small intermediate area reserved for the owner of the house (Java)

Punan forest nomads (Borneo)

pura bale agung 'temple of the great meeting hall' (Bali)

pura dalem 'temple of the unpurified dead' (Bali)

pura desa village temple dedicated to Brahma (Bali)

pura puseh 'temple of origin' (Bali)

rumah adat traditional house

rumah gadang traditional house of the Minangkabau (Sumatra)

rumah lima traditional house, Palembang (Sumatra)

rumah lipat kijang traditional house (Riau)

rumah pasuk Karo house set on pillars driven straight into the ground and cross-braced just below the level of the floor

rumah sangka manuk Karo house set on a rectangular grid of horizontally laid trimmed poles, with the lateral and longitudinal poles set into each other (Sumatra)

rumbia sago palm

rusuk house of a widow or bachelor (Mentawai)

Sa'dan Toraja group (Sulawesi)

Sakuddei indigenous group (Siberut island)

salong Kenyah and Kayan Dayak burial hut (Borneo)

Sasak indigenous group (Lombok)

sasaka Balinese pillar

sentong ceremonial area within a Balinese house

sesat a communal house, Lampung (Sumatra)

Simalungun Batak group (Sumatra)

singa mythical snake- or dragon-like creature, Batak culture

sirih a stimulant of areca-nut, betel leaf and lime

sopo Batak rice barn (Sumatra)

sopo page Karo Batak rice barn (Sumatra)

tanju shaded gallery of an Iban Dayak longhouse

Toba Batak group (Sumatra)

tolak angin angled gable of an Acehnese house (lit. 'shield against the wind')

tongkonan the Toraja word for a 'house of origin', built by the founding ancestor of a clan

Toraja indigenous group (Sulawesi)

udangi Balinese master builder

uma traditional house, particularly in parts of Borneo and Sumatra

uma hai large longhouse built by the Ngaju Dayak of Kalimantan

uma lautem traditional house of Los Palos (Timor)

Yali indigenous group (Irian Jaya)

Bibliography

Barbier, J.P., *Tobaland: The Shreds of Tradition*, 1983

Barbier, J.P., and Douglas Newton, *Islands and Ancestors: Indigenous Styles of South-East Asia*, 1988

Barnes, R., *Kédang: A study of the Collective Thought of an Eastern Indonesian People*, 1974

Clamagirand, B., 'The Ema House (Portuguese Timor)', *Asie du Sud-Est et Monde Insulindien*, 1975

———, 'The Social Organisation of the Ema of Timor', in J.J. Fox (ed.), *The Flow of Life: Essays on Eastern Indonesia*, 1980

———, *Marobo: An Ema Society of Timor*, 1982

Covarrubias, M., *Island of Bali*, 1987

Cunningham, C., 'Order in the Atoni House', *Bijdragen tot de Taal-, Land- en Volkenkunde*, 1964

Dall, G., 'The Traditional Acehnese House', in J. Maxwell (ed.), *The Malay Islamic World of Sumatra*, 1982

Djauhari Sumintardja, 'Looking for a Traditional House of West Java', *Masalah Bangunan*, 18, 1973

———, 'The Badui of West Java: On the Crossroads of Development', *Prisma*, 12, 1973

Domenig, G., *Tectonics in Primitive Roof Construction*, 1980

Drabbe, P., *The Life of the Tanimbarese; Ethnographic Study of the Tanimbarese People*, 1940

Duly, C., *The Houses of Mankind*, 1979

Dumarcay, J., *The House in South-East Asia*, 1985

Feldman, J.A., 'The Architecture of Nias, Indonesia, with Special Reference to Bawomataluo Village', Ph.D. thesis, 1977

———, 'The House as World in Bawomataluo, South Nias', in E. Bruner and J. Becker (eds.), *Art, Ritual and Society in Indonesia*, 1979

———, 'Dutch Galleons and South Nias Palaces', *RES*, 7 (8), 1984

———, *The Eloquent Dead: Ancestral Sculpture of Indonesia and Southeast Asia*, 1985

Fox, J.J., *Harvest of the Palm: Ecological Change in Eastern Indonesia*, 1977

———, *The Flow of Life: Essays on Eastern Indonesia*, 1980

Geertz, H. and C., *Kinship in Bali*, 1975

Gibbs, P., *Building a Malay House*, 1987

Guidoni, E., *Primitive Architecture*, 1978

Hitchcock, M.J., 'Technology and Society in Bima, Sumbawa, with Special Reference to House Building and Textile Manufacture', D. Phil. thesis, 1983

Izikowitz, K. and P. Sorensen (eds.), *The House in East and Southeast Asia: Anthropological and Architectural Aspects*, 1982

Kis-Jovak, J., *Indigenous Architecture of Siberut*, 1980

Kis-Jovak, J., R. Schefold, H. Nooy-Palm and U. Schula-Dornburg, *Banua Toraja: Changing patterns in architecture and symbolism among the Sa'dan Toraja, Sulawesi*, 1988

Lewcock, R. and G. Brans, 'The Boat as an Architectural Symbol', in P. Oliver (ed.), *Shelter, Sign and Symbol*, 1975

Lim Jee Yuan, *The Malay House: Rediscovering Malaysia's Indigenous Shelter System*, 1987

Loeb, E., *Sumatra: Its History and People*, 1935, reprinted 1989

Lubis, M., *Indonesia: Land Under the Rainbow*, 1990

Marsden, W., *The History of Sumatra*, 1966

Nooy-Palm, C.H.M. *et al*, *The Sa'dan Toraja: A Study of Their Social Life and Religion*, Vol 1, 1979

Oliver, P. (ed.), *Shelter and Society*, 1969

——— (ed.), *Shelter, Sign and Symbol*, 1975

——— (ed.), *Dwellings: the House Across the World*, 1987

Roth, H.L., *The Natives of Sarawak and British North Borneo*, 2 vols., 1896, reprinted 1968

Rudofsky, B., *Architecture without Architects*, 1964

Sargeant., G. 'House Form and Decoration in Sumatra', in D. Jones and G. Michell (eds.), *Vernacular Architecture of the Islamic World and Indian Asia*, 1977

Sargeant, G. and R. Saleh, *Traditional Buildings of Indonesia*, Vol 1: *Batak Toba*; Vol. 2: *Batak Karo*; Vol. 3: *Batak Simalungun/Mandailing*, 1973

Schroder, E.E.W.Gs., *Nias, Ethnographical, Geographical and Historical Notes and Studies*, 1917

Schulte Nordholt, H.G., *The Political System of the Atoni of Timor*, 1971

Sellato, B., *Hornbill and Dragon: Arts and Culture of Borneo*, 1989

Sherwin, D., 'From Batak to Minangkabau; An Architectural Trajectory', *Majallah Akitek* 1, 1979

Sibeth, Achim, *The Batak: Peoples of the Island of Sumatra*, 1991

Soebadio, H., 'The Documentary Study of Traditional Balinese Architecture: Some Preliminary Notes', *Indonesian Quarterly*, 3, 1975

Tan, R., 'The Domestic Architecture of South Bali', *Bijdragen tot de taal-, Land- en Volkenkunde*, 1967

Taylor, P.M., and L. Aragon, *Beyond the Java Sea: Art of Indonesia's Outer Islands*, 1991

Tillema, H., *Apo-kajan: A Film Journey To and Through Central Borneo*, 1938

Waterson, R., *The Living House: An Anthropology of Architecture in South-East Asia*, 1990

Index

Numerals in *italic* refer to colour illustration numbers